THE POET'S DEFENCE

CAMBRIDGE
UNIVERSITY PRESS
LONDON: BENTLEY HOUSE
NEW YORK, TORONTO, BOMBAY
CALCUTTA, MADRAS: MACMILLAN
TOKYO: MARUZEN COMPANY LTD

THE POET'S DEFENCE

BY

J. BRONOWSKI

CAMBRIDGE: AT THE UNIVERSITY PRESS

1939

CONTENTS

FOREWORD

FOREWORD

I

JOHN DRYDEN lived at a time when much criticism was written in England. What was written was lively and apt. Yet Dryden was jealous of the better criticism written in France. For Dryden thought well of criticism. He believed that criticism serves the health of poetry.

Dryden's belief has been held by other English poets. It has made them take an uncommon interest in criticism. Some poets have pressed this interest so far that criticism has taken an almost personal turn from them. Sidney, Dryden, Wordsworth are among these. They have written criticism, the best criticism in English. Therefore a study of English criticism must begin at these poets. Perhaps it need go no farther.

I therefore choose as critics some poets, not in order to be odd, nor to give their criticism a weight which it does not have. I choose Dryden and Wordsworth because they are among the great critics. And although Johnson and Arnold said things which we like to hear, they are not among these.

The judgments of Dryden and Wordsworth are worth hearing in themselves. They are also worth hearing because they are made by poets. Dryden and Wordsworth believed that criticism serves the health of poetry. This belief has been debated since. Poetasters have attacked it and criticasters have

defended it. The sides have not remembered that
the belief has been debated by men better fitted to
debate it. What is criticism worth? what is poetry
worth? has been asked and answered by great men
who were both critics and poets. This book sets out
their answers. I have read the answers of critics and
have doubted the use of criticism. I give the answers
of poets because they have taught me the use of
criticism.

I have been urged by another thought. We read
the poems of the past, and we know that we do not
write poems as good. We read the criticism of the
past, and it seems foolish to us. It is spent on dead
matters. It is made with words which are loose and
clumsy to us, and with standards so simple that they
seem to us childish. We are sure that we have better
words and better, scientific standards. We are sure,
even when we see how well the past critics judged
the good and the bad. We see how justly Dryden
praised Shakespeare, and Wordsworth blamed Dryden. What chance made them just if the standards
by which they judged were bad? What is the use
of our good standards if we cannot better the judgments made with bad standards?

Dryden and Wordsworth did not judge well by
chance. They judged well because their spoken and
unspoken standards are better than we understand.
Their standards seem childish because their words
are strange to us. We do not know whether the words
of Dryden or Wordsworth were less supple or less
exact than ours. We do not know because we do

not understand them. For the words of criticism have changed past understanding. Dryden himself wrote of the Ancients,

To admire them as we ought, we should understand them better then we do. Doubtless many things appear flat to us, whose wit depended upon some custome or story which never came to our knowledge, or perhaps upon some Criticism in their language, which being so long dead, and onely remaining in their Books, 'tis not possible they should make us know it perfectly.

If we wish to understand past criticism we must do more than read it. We must believe that its stiff and vague words were once as supple and exact as the words of a science to-day. In this belief we must search for their meanings in the work of the time. We shall not understand what Wit meant to Dryden from his definitions; for their words are also strange to us. We shall only understand it from the poems in which Dryden wrote wittily. We shall only understand what Nature meant to Wordsworth from his poems. That is why the plainest past criticism is the criticism written by poets: because their poems tell us what their words and their standards mean. I have studied the criticism of poets to learn this.

I have held to this end fixedly; and I have perhaps made this book merely a history of the half-dozen words which have been the banners of poets and of critics. One is the word Poetry itself. Another is the word Imagination, which has most often stood in place of Poetry. Two others are the words Virtue and Nature. I have not niggled with the meanings of these words or listed the nigglings of others. Each word has been the core and the symbol of a vast belief of poets. I have looked for these beliefs and for the changes in them. And I have looked for them in these words because the lasting words have stamped the thought of poets. For example, Shelley's *Defence of Poetry* is a frenzied play of the words Poetry and Imagination. And Coleridge's criticism springs from the sudden understanding of such words, which flashes when it is true, but which is often false and shoddy.

I have found the meanings of these words in the work of the poets who used them. It is not to my point that these meanings have often been taken by them from other poets and critics. When Ben Jonson wrote of Nature he borrowed from Horace, Longinus, Aristotle and others. It is not my study how much of their meanings he kept and how much he changed. My study is what he meant; and nothing can tell this but his own writings.

I have kept this book free of the donnish histories of such borrowings. And I have kept it free of the other outfits of scholarship: lists, notes, likenesses, debates with critics. Scholarship is the beginning of a book: it is not an end. I have taken scholarship for granted. For example, I have not listed all the criticism of all poets. Again, I have been content to say that it is likely that Sidney's *Defence of Poesie* was written to answer Gosson's *Schoole of Abuse*, without a show of the reasons which make me sure. There are good reasons to be found in the wording of these pamphlets. But my reason at last is my essay on Sidney: that the two pamphlets debate two beliefs so carefully.

I have pointed only to likenesses which are to my point. I have taken to pieces a line of Dryden,

Till rolling time is lost in round eternity.

I have not reminded the reader that Dryden is thinking of Henry Vaughan's *The World*,

I saw Eternity the other night
Like a great *Ring* of pure and endless light,
    All calm, as it was bright,
And round beneath it, Time in hours, days, years
    Driv'n by the spheres
Like a vast shadow mov'd.

For the likeness tells nothing about Dryden's belief. But I have underlined the likeness between the climaxes of *Prometheus Unbound* and *The Rime of the Ancient Mariner*, because it sums the likeness of Shelley's and Coleridge's beliefs.

These beliefs are my study. I have tried to say nothing about the belief of a poet which I have not said in his own words. I have looked closely at the words which I have quoted. I have followed their meaning to the end. Some readers will think that the care with which I have followed the meaning is out of place. They will think that the words of Shelley or of Swinburne must not be followed too reasonably. These readers do not deny that Shelley and Swinburne meant what I reason that they meant. They merely deny that Shelley and Swinburne knew that they meant this, and that they wanted to mean this. They grant that Shelley and Swinburne shut their eyes to their own beliefs; and they ask us also to shut our eyes. I do not know why we should do so. Criticism means something and poems mean something; and I do not know why we should stop half-way through their meanings. I have tried to follow each meaning to its end. I have tried to give each meaning the care which I can. And in turn I have tried to put my meaning as barely and to follow it as far as I can. Criticism has too long helped itself with false poetic tricks and with vague words, Value, Form, Content. I have tried to write without tricks and without these words. I praise the criticism of poets. But the fault of criticism is that it has been written by would-be poets. I have tried to write criticism as reasoned as geometry.

2

So much for the manner of this book. What of its matter? What are the beliefs which I have found behind the large words of poets?

I have found that the beliefs have changed less than the words. I think that the best poets have had some beliefs in common; and that poets have written worse as they have lost these beliefs. One belief is that poetry is worthy in itself. Another is that this worth must be judged, not measured. That is, this worth cannot be abstracted from the poem like the wavelength of a light from its colour, and given a measure. It must be judged, as it must be made, by the whole soul of man. That is why great criticism, like great poems, has not been written by little men.

This belief has been denied by Coleridge and now by his pupil I. A. Richards. They have found a measure of worth in the measures of pleasure psychology. There are others who have seemed to grant the belief, against whom this book is also written. These are writers like Swinburne who say that because worth cannot be measured, it cannot be judged at all. They say that each man must be allowed what he likes. No poem is good or bad. It is merely good for something, bad for someone.

Both sets of writers share an unspoken belief: that only that can be judged which can be measured. It is the belief that science is the only way to knowledge. This belief has grown as science has grown wider. From the hopes of the Augustans it has grown to the boundless pride of to-day. I do not think that it is chance that poets have grown so much worse in the same time.

Peacock said that poets were growing worse because they were growing out of date. He said that poems have no place in a more and more scientific society. This may be true: this book does not deny it. The belief in the worth of poetry, which I read in great poets, may be false. If it is, we must put up with losing poetry for the sake of winning true beliefs. And I should count the gain greater than the loss.

I hope that this book makes plain that I believe in one worth only: Truth. I defend poetry because I think that it tells the truth.

In science, that is true which can be checked by others. Science therefore finds its knowledge of the world by mass measurement, that is by social means. It finds it through the senses, and what it finds is never true but more and more nearly true. This holds of physics, of history, and also of psychology. Psychology studies the mind of man: but it can study it only in the conduct of men. It must set the words and deeds of one man by those of another, it must find what conduct he shares with others in his society and in other societies. It can read a mind only behind these masks. And the mind which it reads is a mind within society.

But I believe that there is truth which is not reached by these means. I believe that there is truth which is free of the society within which it has been found. I believe that the mind of man has a steady shape which is the truth. We know the truth about the mind by looking from this *a priori* truth outward. No scientific near-truths and nearer-truths can give this shape as we can give it ourselves. The rules of reasoning are part of this steady shape without which the mind cannot be. For formal logics may change, but the rules of reasoning are steady now as in Egypt, and here as in Greenland. The urges of passion are part of the steady shape of the mind. All these are true in all societies. They make an absolute truth, which I think is the truth of poetry.

I believe in ideal truth. The word Ideal is in bad odour to-day, and rightly so; and I wish that I could have found another word. For the word has been used to hide all that is meanest in the conduct of men. An ideal has commonly been something for whose sake men have been asked to go hungry. I ask no one to go hungry. I believe that we cannot think of ideals until we are fed. And perhaps we should not talk about ideals until we are all fed. I am willing to believe that I who wrote this book, and you who read it, would be doing better to fight for a world in which we shall all be fed. I underline that I am a materialist in politics as I am in science and in all social life. Because social living is material living, and anyone who tries to dress it with ideals is only the cover for someone who will ask us to go hungry.

I believe that ideals and social living are two different fields. But social living is not the whole life of man. It is all his life of sense and his life in the world. It is not all his life in the mind. The mind of man has a knowledge of truth beyond the near-truths of science and society. I believe that poetry tells this truth.

I have set out this belief in this book, and most plainly in what I have written on Sidney. Sidney sees that the written poem is always something of a travesty of its ideal, because it is written through the senses. But he stresses that no ideal can be written of in any other way. And for Sidney the ideal flashes also over living in the moments of greatest living.

This is the Renaissance belief; and it has dangers. For the moments of great living are social moments: and then Sidney's ideal of Virtue is abused, when it is brought into the social life. The Elizabethans did abuse their ideals. Nevertheless they made the belief which has made English poetry.

Against Sidney I have set Shelley. I have gone thus out of the order of time and the slow change of belief, because I have wanted to put plainly the two beliefs which are at odds. Shelley is commonly taken to be an idealist because he is vague and hopeful. I have been at pains to show that Shelley has no ideal. Shelley held vaguely to poetry because he liked it; but his faith was in science because he was in awe of it. Shelley's *Defence of Poetry* is at last, that the poet is a kind of scientist, and even is a better scientist than scientists.

I do not think that poetry can be defended with such fancies. If we believe that only science can tell the truth, I think that it is our business to get on with being scientists. If we believe this and are still poets, we are holding up the world as grossly as those who burn books or coffee. We may find excuses for poetry: as a makeshift propaganda until science has found a better, as a makeshift training of the will until science has found a better. But these are only excuses for doing what we like. We should be learning about propaganda and the will as sciences; and we should face the knowledge that poetry is doomed.

The break between Sidney and Shelley did not come all at once. It grew for two hundred and fifty years. I have followed its growth through Dryden, Wordsworth and Coleridge, and then beyond Shelley. I have found the belief in the ideal in Dryden, and something of the belief in Wordsworth. The ideal has changed in them. In both it is called Nature. I think that Dryden means by this the root mind of man, and Wordsworth means the root passions of man. Dryden thinks of this Nature as made by the mind, and Wordsworth thinks of it as given to the mind. But this difference is less than the likeness: that both set Nature away from the senses, and both find it true by standards greater than the social tests. Dryden held his Nature to the end. It did not sink to the silliness of the Augustans until he died. Wordsworth failed at last to keep his Nature away from the nature of the senses. When he failed, after the *Intimations of Immortality*, he stopped writing true poems. It is ironical that he quarrelled with Coleridge then, when he was about to follow Coleridge into the social world of the nineteenth century.

From Coleridge I have traced a set of mock idealists not unlike Shelley: Swinburne and his heirs. They believe that poetry cannot be spoken about at all. They believe that we can only like or dislike a poem and we cannot say what we like or dislike in it. This is the mock ideal of 'pure' poetry and of Art for Art's Sake. I have been at pains as great to overthrow this as the mock ideal of Shelley. The worth of poetry cannot be measured, but it can be judged: and we can know what we are judging. We do not come to poetry by running from life. Poetry is not a negative, a desert island. We come to poetry by looking for truth, and poetry is a positive truth.

I think that almost all great poets have held to this ideal of poetry. Some readers may think that no great poems have been written without this ideal. I should have thought this but for the example of W. B. Yeats. I read Yeats as a worldly poet, but I think that he is a great poet. I think that his is the last anti-poetic faith, and stands against poetry. It is just to end this book with his name.

3

What is the ideal which poets have held? It is an ideal which they have not seen alike. Dryden saw it as the root mind of man, Wordsworth as his root passion, Sidney as his Virtue. These ideals have only this in common, that each is set against the worldly and social life of men. They do call on man's thoughts and man's passions, but they call on them as roots of all thought and passion: not as the thoughts and passions of this man or that. They are more than the thoughts and passions common to men; they are part of the shape of man's mind. These ideals rest on man as he is himself, and as surely rest outside what man must always be. I quote Sidney,

Our erected wit maketh us know what perfectiõ is, and yet our infected wil keepeth us frõ reaching unto it.

A poetry whose ideal is, to be set against the worldly life of man, can only teach man to hold to an ideal, the truth. It can teach man nothing about his social life. I do not mean that poems do not teach worldly knowledge. Poems have many things in them beside poetry. Poems delight the senses. They are also good carriers of propaganda and of much by-the-way knowledge. And no poem will reach us which does not carry such knowledge. No poet will write well who does not write with worldly knowledge and aptness. But poetry is in none of these. Poetry is carried by the sensuous and worldly aptness of the poem, but it is an ideal set against the senses and against worldly life. Its standards are not standards of living.

For example, we ask of a prose speech that it shall have the virtues of common speech: it shall be understandable, exact, and moving. We ask this because we have in mind the end which speech is to serve. But poetry is what Sidney called 'an other nature'. It does not serve the ends of speech, and we do not ask it to be common speech. Many of us are content to find a poem only partly understandable, and most of us take for granted that it will be inexact. And therefore poems cannot teach us these worldly goods, to be understandable, to be exact.

Some readers will say that poetry serves the feelings; but otherwise is not unlike most worldly living. They will recall that we ask both prose and poetry to be moving. They will say that poems, which are often moving, are thus linked to life, which is sometimes moving. This answer does not go deep enough. For when we say that a speech is moving, we have in mind a deed or purpose towards which we are being moved. This is not how we ask poems to move us. Aristotle said that tragedy moves us—or purges us: the metaphor is the same—by way of pity and terror. The sentence shows that Aristotle saw poetry as an end outside worldly living. For if Aristotle had been told that an everyday worldly speech, say by Judge Jeffreys, moved us by pity and terror, he would have asked, Does it move us to be just or unjust? Poetry does not move us to be just or unjust, in itself. It moves us to thoughts in whose light justice and injustice are seen in fearful sharpness of outline.

Great poets have thought that poetry is its own end. Had they thought otherwise they would have turned to something which is an end. Only small poets like Shelley have held to poetry although they have not thought it an end. Great poets have thought that criticism serves the end of poetry. I hope that this book serves the end of poetry. I have written it in the face of so much else to be done in the world, because I have wished to be truthful. What truth do I claim for this book? I claim only a worldly and scientific truth. Criticism serves the truth of poetry, but it cannot have the truth of poetry. Criticism has only social truth, and little of that. For criticism serves poetry at last by pointing to the places where the truth can be found in poems. To do this criticism can only tell near-truths, and does tell lies. The test of criticism is not to be true, but to judge well and to point to truth. I ask this judgment only for my criticism: that it judges poets truly, and that it makes poetry plain as the truth.

SIDNEY & SHELLEY

PHILIP SIDNEY

I

Philip Sidney's fame is not the fame of a poet. The *Arcadia* lives only the dusty life of Lyly's *Euphues*: it is remembered as history, not poetry. Sidney's sonnets have not kept it fresh. Sidney's fame has been kept fresh partly by the *Defence of Poesie*. But more lasting than this has been the memory of Sidney the Elizabethan gallant. Philip Sidney, Knight, was a man of uncommon delights, eagerness, and single mind. These virtues filled his acts, and fill his writings. The *Defence of Poesie* takes these virtues to be the commonplace of poems, and of every life. This is the faith which makes the *Defence* so winning an appeal. The man, rather than any principle, is winning; and the man has the graces of humour and liveliness. In this way, as a piece of graceful and manly pleading, the *Defence of Poesie* has helped to make Sidney's fame the fame of a gallant.

Nevertheless, Sidney was a poet. Sidney, the poet of *Astrophel and Stella*, is not a gallant. He is a serious poet. Few English poems before Sidney's have his seriousness: a speaking by the poet himself to his self. Sidney's poems have only a beginning of it. We must not judge them by poems in which this way of speaking has become the only way: by Wordsworth's *Lucy* poems, or by the love poems of Burns. But *Astrophel and Stella* is serious enough to mark principles in

Sidney, which make the *Defence of Poesie* all at once purposeful writing.

It is likely that the *Defence of Poesie* was written to answer a pamphlet by Stephen Gosson called *The Schoole of Abuse*, which had been dedicated to Sidney. The greater part of *The Schoole of Abuse* is an attack upon plays and playhouses. Before this main attack, Gosson makes some charges against poetry. None of these charges is weighty or new. But they are shrewdly put together, to make a case which Sidney did not find easy to answer.

The case is made up of three charges, and a precedent. Sidney, more orderly than Gosson, gives a list of them in the *Defence of Poesie*.

First, that there beeing manie other more frutefull knowledges, a man might better spend his time in them, then in this. Secondly, that it is the mother of lyes. Thirdly, that it is the nurse of abuse, infecting us with many pestilent desires, with a *Sirens* sweetnesse, drawing the minde to the Serpents taile of sinfull fansies.

And lastly and chiefly, they cry out with open mouth as if they had overshot *Robinhood*, that *Plato* banished them out of his Commonwealth.

But this list is made with an eye to the answers. Gosson did not group the charges in this way; and Gosson gave them other stresses.

The charge which Gosson stresses is the third. He speaks the key word to it in his first sentences, when he says with scorn that poets are 'amarous'. The word stands at the head of two trains of thought. On one hand, the poet leads his readers to wantonness;

this alone is the third charge in Sidney's list. On
the other hand, he comes to do this because he

> dwelleth longest in those pointes, that profite least.

Gosson is pointing to a force in the poet's writing
which is graver than any effect on a reader. The
examples which he gives,

> *Virgill* sweates in describyng his Gnat: *Ouid* bestirreth
> him to paint out his Flea,

may even be to show that it is a force which masters
the poet's will. This is the nature of poetry, Gosson
holds: to take for matter that which profits least.
Sidney in his list bundles this charge with the first
charge. To do so is to allow it only the narrow meaning
of another and lesser charge of Gosson's,

> If people will bee instructed, (God be thanked) wee
> haue Diuines enough to discharge that, and moe by
> a great many, then are well hearkened to:

the meaning that there are better knowledges than
poetry, and better ways of getting knowledge than
from poems. This is not Gosson's charge in its wide
meaning. Gosson charges poetry with being by nature
drawn from what is fruitless. It merely follows that
poems will lead the reader astray, and that he had
better learn elsewhere. And Gosson makes it follow
closely. Exactly that it does follow, and that the
charges can thus be linked as one, Sidney's orderly
list is meant to deny.

We can read this spoiling tactic in the second
charge of Sidney's list: that poetry 'is the mother of

lyes'. Gosson does not say this. He does call poets
'fathers of lyes'. He says how they lie, and to what
end.

> Many good sentences are spoken by *Danus*, to shadowe
> his knauery: and written by Poets, as ornamentes to
> beautifye their woorkes, and sette theyr trumperie too
> sale without suspect.

> Pul off the visard that Poets maske in, you shall disclose
> their reproch, bewray their vanitie, loth their wanton-
> nesse, lament their follie, and perceiue their sharpe sayings
> to be placed as Pearles in Dunghils, fresh pictures on
> rotten walles, chaste Matrons apparel on common Cur-
> tesans. These are the Cuppes of *Circes*, that turne reason-
> able Creatures into brute Beastes.

On both sides, this charge is linked to Gosson's main
charge that poets are 'amarous'. It makes the points
of that double charge, that their matter is bad and
their end is to breed wantonness. But when Sidney
comes to answer the charge that poetry 'is the mother
of lyes', he reads it quite unlike this. He reads it as
a charge that the stories told by poets are lies; and
answers easily that they are not lies but fables.
Gosson had not said that poets tell lying stories. He
had said how poets lie, and why. Sidney's sleight of
hand with the happy phrase, 'the mother of lyes',
does not answer his charge.

Why does Sidney shirk Gosson's charges in this
way? What is the force in them which he will not
meet? I have said that it is not the force of any one
charge, but of the way in which they are linked.
I have taken as key word to the thought which links
them Gosson's word of scorn, 'amarous'. The meaning

of the word in these charges is clear; it is apt to
quote the same meaning from Milton, who writes of

no serious Book, but the vain amatorious Poem of Sr
Philip Sidneys Arcadia.

Milton's meaning is given by the word vain as much
as by the word amatorious; just as Gosson taxes
amorous poets, that they 'dwell longest in those
pointes, that profite least'. Both mean that poetry
is a fruitless work. Men gain nothing from reading
poetry; and poetry, in mastering them, overthrows
their knowledge of virtue. This is the mastery which
Gosson fears when he writes,

These are the Cuppes of *Circes*, that turne reasonable
Creatures into brute Beastes.

And this is the mastery which Milton fears when he
goes on to call the *Arcadia*

a Book in that kind full of worth and witt, but among
religious thoughts, and duties not worthy to be nam'd; nor
to be read at any time without good caution.

Poetry is not serious: it makes virtue seem a trifling
thing, and so overthrows it.

This is the deeper charge which runs under Gosson's
Schoole of Abuse; which Sidney shirks in making his
list. I read its force, in Milton and in Gosson, in
the word 'amarous'. The charge made by this word,
if it is read alone, does not seem weighty. For it is
a charge only against the subject matter of poets:
it goes no deeper than to say that poets do not write
of grave matters. Read in one way, all Gosson's
charges lay a like stress on the subject of poets: that

they 'dwell longest in those pointes, that profite least'. This stress seems to us misplaced. To-day we hardly take seriously the charge that poets do not write of grave matters. We should bear in mind that when Gosson wrote it was a serious, because it was a just charge. When Gosson wrote, none of the grave English poems which we now know had been written. Of course, when Gosson wrote, few English poems of any kind which we now know had been written. But also the Italian, Latin, and Greek poems which Gosson knew did earn the word of scorn, 'amarous'. So above all did the plays, English and others, which Gosson knew; I recall that *The Schoole of Abuse* was aimed at these.

We think it a ready answer to this, to say that the subject of poems has little to do with the nature of poetry. Sidney also has to make this answer, and is not happy to make it. For it is an answer only if we can point to the many subjects which different poems take for their matter. At a time when almost all poems treat only one subject, love, it is no answer. Gosson could hold with reason that the subject which all poets thought apt and worthy must be bound to poetry by nature. Sidney, looking for poems which take their matter elsewhere, can only claim the bible as poetry; and draw the sting of Gosson's charge, by blaming the poets of his time for their lack of graveness as fiercely as Gosson had done.

Nevertheless, the stress which Gosson puts on the subject matter of poems has this weakness: that it makes a charge against the poets of one time, rather

than against poetry. Even in the poems which Gosson
knew, there were some whose subject was not love:
those Greek and Latin poems whose subject was war.
Since Gosson held that to be warlike is a virtue, which
plays had sapped, he must speak well of these poems,
and set them as patterns of poetry. He must say,

The right vse of auncient Poetrie was too haue the
notable exploytes of woorthy Captaines, the holesome
councels of good fathers, and vertuous liues of predecessors set downe in numbers, and song to the Instrument
at solemne feastes, that the sound of the one might draw
the hearers from kissing the cupp too often; the sense
of the other put them in minde of things past, and chaulk
out the way to do the like.

But to allow such a right use of poetry is to take the
greater force from his charges. For the force of these
charges is that poetry is bad in itself, however it
may be used. If there is a right use of poetry, then
poetry is bad only in being wrongly used. And it is
surely no charge against poetry to say that it may be
wrongly used. Gosson is no longer charging poetry,
but those who use poetry wrongly: the poets of his
own time.

Plutarch reporteth that as *Chiron* was a wise man, a
learned Poet, a skilful Musition, so was hee also a teacher
of iustice, by shewing what Princes ought to doe, and
a Reader of Phisicke, by opening the natures of manie
simples. If you enquire howe manie suche Poetes and
Pipers wee haue in our Age, I am perswaded that euerie
one of them may creepe through a ring, or daunce the
wilde Morice in a Needles eye. We haue infinite Poets,
and Pipers, and suche peeuishe cattel among vs in
Englande, that liue by merrie begging, mainteyned by

almes, and priuily encroch vppon euerie mans purse. But
if they that are in authoritie, and haue the sworde in
their handes to cut off abuses, shoulde call an accompt to
see how many *Chirons*, *Terpandri*, and *Homers* are heere,
they might cast the summe without pen, or counters,
and sit downe with *Racha*, to weepe for her Children,
because they were not.

Gosson is willing thus to narrow his charges, because
The Schoole of Abuse is aimed at the plays of his time.
The narrowing is a weakness in Gosson's charges.
But we must not think it a battle won for poetry.
Gosson charges poetry only by the way. His attack
is on plays and playhouses. If by giving a point to
poetry he can make a point against plays, it is his
business to do so. The sentences I have quoted use
this tactic neatly. They speak highly of poets as they
might be, in order to belittle players as they are. We
should see that this is a point for poetry; but we should
not overrate the reasons which made Gosson yield it.

Sidney in the *Defence of Poesie* as neatly takes the
point which Gosson has yielded. He uses it to meet
the third charge in his list: that poetry 'is the nurse
of abuse, infecting us with many pestilent desires'.

I will not denie, but that mans wit may make *Poesie*,
which should be εἰκαστικὴ, which some learned haue
defined figuring foorth good things to be φανταστικὴ: which
doth contrariwise infect the fancie with unworthy objects.

But what, shal the abuse of a thing, make the right
use odious? Nay truly, though I yeeld, that *Poesie* may
not onely be abused, but that being abused by the reason
of his sweete charming force, it can do more hurt then
anie other armie of words: yet shall it be so farre from
concluding, that the abuse should give reproach to the

abused, that cõtrariwise, it is a good reason, that whatsoever being abused, doth most harme, being rightly used
(and upon the right use, ech thing receives his title)
doth most good.

The reasoning is not so good as Sidney claims; but
it is apt, and it makes the debating points. Gosson
has allowed that there is a right use of poetry. Sidney
does not let the point go. He joins Gosson in blaming
those who use poetry wrongly, in order to praise the
more righteously those who use it well; and to make
the higher claims for their uses. And Sidney takes
the argument farther, against Gosson's last attack,
the precedent 'that *Plato* banished them out of his
Commonwealth'. For Plato did not mean poets in
general, says Sidney; he meant only those poets who
belittle the gods. Thus Plato also did not charge
poetry, but those poets who abuse poetry.

S. Paul himselfe sets a watch-word uppon *Philosophie*,
indeed uppon the abuse. So doth *Plato* uppon the abuse,
not upon *Poetrie*.

So as *Plato* banishing the abuse, not the thing, not
banishing it, but giving due honour to it, shall be our
Patron, and not our adversarie.

This is to make the most of the point which Gosson
has yielded; but to make it in the face of truth. We
may doubt what Plato meant when he banished poets
from his commonwealth. We cannot doubt that he
banished them for being poets. To say that he
banished them merely for belittling the gods, or for
putting about any other belief, is plainly false. Plato
banished poets because the state of mind to which

poetry is a good was out of place in his antiseptic commonwealth. Plato's is a commonwealth of reason. The commonwealth of which Renaissance writers thought, the commonwealth of Thomas More for example, is a commonwealth of reasonableness. Those who live in More's commonwealth are allowed any reasonable pleasure, such as poetry. Those who live in Plato's commonwealth are allowed only reasoned pleasures; and poetry is not a reasoned pleasure. Renaissance writers tried to think of Plato's *Republic* as if it were More's homely *Utopia*, or even the gallant *Arcadia* of Sidney. They were then put to odd shifts to hide the unlikeness of these commonwealths. When Sidney says that Plato banished poets merely because he thought that they belittle the gods, he has been put to such a shift. To Sidney, the *Republic* is an authority which cannot be overthrown. It is not merely a political plan, but an ideal. Unlike Sidney, we should read the *Republic* as politics: the plan of a commonwealth whose policy is made by reason alone. In such a *Republic* the banishing of poets is good politics: because the thoughts which move them and with which they move others are counter to the policy of the commonwealth. Since Sidney will not read it thus, he has no truthful answer to Gosson's quoting of the *Republic*.

The answer which Sidney makes is that Plato banished only the abuse of poetry. I have said that this is false. In Plato's commonwealth, poetry is itself an abuse: the abuse of reason. If Plato banished poetry for its abuses, they are abuses which are bound

into poetry so that they cannot be unravelled; they
are in the nature of poetry. To Gosson also, the abuses
of poetry are of this kind. There is a right use of
poetry, Gosson says; but even if this right use is made,
it is bound to abuses which outweigh it. The abuses
cannot in nature be stripped from poetry.

Anacharsis being demaunded of a *Greeke*, whether they
had not instrumentes of Musicke, or Schooles of Poetrie
in *Scythia*, answered, yes, and that without vice, as though
it were either impossible, or incredible, that no abuse
should be learned where such lessons are taught, and
such schooles mainteined.

And that Gosson did think it either impossible, or
incredible, we learn from his own note to this sentence,

Poetrie in *Scythia* without vice, as the *Phœnix* in *Arabia*,
without a fellow.

The nature of poetry is to carry abuses, as surely as
the nature of birds is to die. If there is a poetry
without abuse, it is such a freak as the deathless
Phœnix.

This is the charge which Gosson has made already,
in its simple form: that poetry by nature overthrows
virtue. He makes it here in a form which is apt.
He had yielded the point, that there is a right use of
poetry; and we have seen that Sidney uses the point
to the full. Now we see that Gosson has guarded
against the answers for which Sidney uses it. For he
claims that poetry cannot be unbound from its abuses;
and if this is true, 'the right vse of auncient Poetrie'
is a phrase, upheld by no known poems, at most

a hope for poetry. The quarrel here between Gosson and Sidney therefore hangs on the meaning which they give to the words, the right use. Gosson changes that meaning as he writes, for his own ends; the sleight of hand is like Sidney's sleight with the phrase 'the mother of lyes'. Gosson writes,

The right vse of auncient Poetrie was too haue the notable exploytes of woorthy Captaines, the holesome councels of good fathers, and vertuous liues of predecessors set downe in numbers, and song to the Instrument at solemne feastes.

After this maner were the *Bœotians* trained from rudenesse to ciuilitie, The *Lacedæmonians* instructed by *Tyrteæus* verse, The *Argiues* by the melody of *Telesilla*, And the *Lesbians* by *Alcæus* Odes.

The right use which he means here is an actual use. The poems which he quotes may be lost, or may be fabled poems which had never been written; but Gosson is thinking of them as actual poems, and of their use as a use by men who lived. This is not the right use which he means when he writes that

it were either impossible, or incredible, that no abuse should be learned where such lessons are taught.

Here the abuse is held to be in the nature of poetry; and a right use of poetry is therefore an ideal use, which no actual poem can make. The poet has in mind a right use of poetry; but the act of writing the poem damages his ideal, and makes abuses. When Gosson allows that there is a right use of poetry, he means an actual use. When he hedges the ground which he has yielded, he shifts his meaning to an ideal use. This tactic should not be passed over. But neither should it make us forget that Gosson's case is sound. For the right use which Gosson quotes in the poems of the Bœotians, the Lacedæmonians, the Argives, is a fabled use. We know nothing of it but hearsay. Gosson himself would not have allowed it as an actual use, had he not been trying to make another point. It is his tactic here to speak highly of poets as they are said to have been, in order to belittle them as they are. This is only a debating point, which we can discount. But if we discount it, we cannot claim that the right uses which Gosson allows are actual uses. Gosson's case is then bare, and strongest. There is an ideal right use of poetry, in the mind of the poet. But this is not the use made by any actual poem, because the very writing of the poem makes abuses. There are therefore no poems which do not carry abuses, in their nature.

We now see that Sidney does not answer this charge at all. Tactically, he makes the most of what Gosson has allowed: that there is a right use of poetry, and that it is the abuses of poetry which are at fault. He answers, 'But what, shal the abuse of a thing, make the right use odious?' and 'Upon the right use, ech thing receives his title'. This answer has force only if that right use is an actual use; and this is the meaning which Sidney gives to the words, the right use. With this meaning, it is just to claim that poetry must be judged by its right use. But if the right use is not an actual use, poetry cannot claim to be judged by it. For there is then no poem which

is free from abuse; and the abuse does make every
actual use odious. Sidney can claim that poetry
should not be judged by its abuses, only if he can
point to poems which are free from abuse. He points
to none. The list of poems which Gosson had given
is clearly worthless. We have only fragments of
Alcæus, Tyrtæus, Terpander; Chiron is a fable; all we
know of these poets is hearsay. Lamely, Sidney claims
the bible as poetry. In English poetry, he can praise
only four poems: *Troilus and Criseyde*, the *Mirror for
Magistrates*, the Earl of Surrey's lyrics, and the *Shep-
heardes Calender*. None of these is without the abuses
against which Gosson wrote, and even their matter is
the 'amarous' matter which he scorned. For the rest,
Sidney must blame English poets as fiercely as Gosson
had done. Thus he has no actual right use of poetry
to set against the ideal use of which Gosson wrote;
and no answer to Gosson's charge, that the abuses
of poetry are bound in its nature. When Gosson wrote,
there was in the end no answer to the mocking note
which he set in his margin,

Poetrie in *Scythia* without vice, as the *Phœnix* in *Arabia*,
without a fellow.

2

I have set out Gosson's charges and the answers to
them which Sidney made. The charges take their
strength from the way in which they are linked, upon
one common thought. I have been at pains to under-

line their strength, and the weakness of Sidney's answers. It is easy to belittle Gosson, and to overrate Sidney's answers. *The Schoole of Abuse* now seems to us merely sprightly, if we read it at all; we do not understand Gosson's passionate Puritan wit, and we care nothing for his case. *The Defence of Poesie* is graver, and we do care for Sidney's case. Sidney's case is a good case. But we shall not see its worth unless we understand the strength of Gosson's case: and that Gosson cannot be fobbed off with the answers which I have quoted from Sidney. Gosson's charges are based on one principle. Sidney's answers cannot shake them, except as they are based on a principle as firm as Gosson's. Only this principle makes the worth of the *Defence of Poesie*.

I recall the charges which Sidney did not answer. Their key is the charge that poetry, 'amarous', by nature 'dwelleth longest in those pointes, that profite least'. Even if we read this as a charge only against the subject matter of poems, in Sidney's time it could not be answered. But it is more than a charge against the poets of that time. It sets the abuse of poetry in that time against a right use of poetry; but it makes the right use an ideal use, which cannot be freed from its actual abuses. The principle on which Gosson's charges are based is therefore a single theory of poetry. In this theory, the right use of poetry is an ideal in the mind of the poet. But the very writing of the poem damages the ideal, and makes abuses. For the writing of the poem is an act of the senses: the poem pleases, and moves, through the senses;

and the senses damage the virtue of the mind. The right use of poetry is in the mind; the abuses of poems are made by the senses, and cannot be stripped from poetry. Gosson puts this theory into a simple likeness:

I may well liken *Homer* to *Mithecus*, and Poets to Cookes the pleasures of the one winnes the body from labor, and conquereth the sense; the allurement of the other drawes the mind from vertue, and confoundeth wit.

The pleasures of the poem are pleasures of the senses; and they master the mind's ideal.

These are the Cuppes of *Circes*, that turne reasonable Creatures into brute Beastes.

In that part of the *Defence of Poesie* in which Sidney has set himself to strike at these charges singly, with any weapon to hand, he has failed. The greater part of the *Defence of Poesie*, however, does not answer Gosson's single charges. It sets out Sidney's own account of poetry.

Sidney's account begins with a history of poetry, which is fanciful, but which makes two pointed claims. Sidney claims that poets were the 'Fathers in learning', in whom began all knowledge. And he claims that in poems there has always been read something more than manly, something prophetic or godly: for this reason prophecies have been spoken in poems. These historical claims do not seem to bear on the nature of poetry, or on its use in Sidney's time. They do bear on the theory of poetry which Sidney is setting up. I recall Gosson's lesser charge which Sidney puts

first in his list, that there are better knowledges than
poetry, and better ways of getting knowledge than from
poems. Sidney's first claim is set against this charge:
and points the way which Sidney means to take. It
claims only that poets were the beginners of knowledge; but it foreshadows the claim that poetry is the
best knowledge. Sidney will not take the meaning
which Gosson has given to the word Knowledge. And
Sidney's second claim foreshadows his meaning.
Sidney's meaning will make of poetry a knowledge
as prophetic, and godly, as the Puritan knowledge
of Gosson and Milton.

In order to make his meaning, Sidney sets out the
scope of the knowledge which the sciences seek, and
the matter which is proper to their knowledge. What
he claims here is at once so artless, and so far-reaching,
that I must quote it at length.

There is no Art delivered unto mankind that hath not
the workes of nature for his principall object, without
which they could not consist, and on which they so
depend, as they become Actors & Plaiers, as it were of
what nature will have set forth. So doth the *Astronomer*
looke upon the starres, and by that he seeth set downe
what order nature hath taken therein. So doth the
Geometritian & *Arithmititian*, in their divers sorts of quan-
tities. So doth the *Musitians* in times tel you, which by
nature agree, which not. The natural *Philosopher* thereon
hath his name, and the morall *Philosopher* standeth uppon
the naturall vertues, vices, or passions of man: and follow
nature saith he therein, and thou shalt not erre.

And the *Metaphisicke* though it be in the second &
abstract Notions, and therefore be counted supernaturall,
yet doth hee indeed build upon the depth of nature.
Onely the Poet disdeining to be tied to any such subjectiŏ,

lifted up with the vigor of his own invention, doth grow
in effect into an other nature: in making things either
better then nature bringeth foorth, or quite a new, formes
such as never were in nature: as the *Heroes*, *Demigods*,
Cyclops, *Chymeras*, *Furies*, and such like; so as he goeth
hand in hand with nature, not enclosed within the narrow
warrant of her gifts, but freely raunging within the Zodiack
of his owne wit.

This is the classical claim that the poet is 'ποιητής,
a Maker' made so simply that it is disarming. It
claims that a poet makes that which he imagines,
absolutely, as nature makes a plant; and that the
poet makes it himself. If there is a greater, making
force working through the poet, it is a godlike force
and not the force of nature. I close the quotation
with the sentence which is the core of the *Defence of
Poesie*.

Neither let it be deemed too sawcy a comparison, to
ballance the highest point of mans wit, with the efficacie
of nature: but rather give right honor to the heavenly
maker of that maker, who having made man to his owne
likenes, set him beyond and over all the workes of that
second nature, which in nothing he sheweth so much as
in Poetry; when with the force of a divine breath, he
bringeth things foorth surpassing her doings: with no
small arguments to the incredulous of that first accursed
fall of *Adam*, since our erected wit maketh us know what
perfectiŏ is, and yet our infected wil keepeth us frŏ
reaching unto it.

This is the theory of poetry which Sidney sets
against Gosson's theory. I have said that in order to
understand it, we must understand the meaning which
Sidney gives to the word Knowledge. We see that this

meaning is still a step away: it lies beyond Sidney's meaning of the word Nature. As Sidney understands it, nature is made by God. What man makes, in a worldly, natural way, is made by nature through man. The knowledge which he makes in the sciences is thus a knowledge of nature, and shaped by nature. But man also has a gift of making which is not worldly. When he uses this gift, the godly force works through him directly; and makes 'an other nature', not shaped by the known nature. This gift is the gift of poetry.

This is a claim unlike the claims which Gosson and Sidney have argued hitherto. It is unlike them in kind: so that Sidney says of it at once, almost with pride, that it 'will by few be understood, and by fewer graunted'. What has been argued is the wantonness bred by poems, their fruitless matter, their actual abuses and right uses. Sidney himself kept the argument on this narrow ground: it was he who would not argue the ideal meaning of the phrase, the right use of poetry, which Gosson sought to give to it. Now Sidney makes claims which are quite outside the range of actual right uses and wrong uses. Sidney is claiming not that poetry does good, but that poetry is good: and more, that poetry is the good. What has been argued hitherto is, How does the reading of poems affect the conduct of men? Is poetry an evil guide for conduct; or can it be used for good? Now Sidney puts aside the standards of good conduct; and claims that poetry is a standard of good, absolute in itself: towards which good conduct and right thinking merely look.

The absolute good which Sidney sees in poetry is the good given by God. Man must get this good from God at first hand; he cannot learn it at second hand through nature. For nature can teach only good conduct: this is Sidney's point when he writes that, in contrast to the poet,

the morall *Philosopher* standeth uppon the naturall vertues, vices, or passions of man: and follow nature saith he therein, and thou shalt not erre.

The only source of absolute good from which man can draw is therefore the books inspired by God at first hand, and not through the hand of nature. Gosson, and Milton, allowed one such book, the bible. Sidney claims an equal place for the books of poets; we now understand why elsewhere he presses the claim that the bible is poetry. To Sidney, God speaks through poets, almost as he speaks through his prophets. This speech makes poems, like the bible, the source of absolute good. Only the word 'almost' spoils the likeness.

It is striking how close this theory is to Gosson's theory. Gosson's charges against poets, and the like charges I have quoted from Milton, are Puritan charges. When we think how we should answer them, we find ourselves denying the very base of the charges. Gosson charges that poets do not write of grave matters: we deny that the good life dwells only in grave matters. Sidney did try to make this kind of answer, and failed. Now that he answers from his own principle, we see that this principle is built on the same bases as Gosson's. His good life is indeed not Gosson's good life. But the good which he sees, and which he seeks to image in his life, is the absolute good to which Gosson holds. Sidney's theory has the bases of Puritan theory. It sets up an ideal good. It sets the giver of this good beyond nature. It sets the good against nature.

Sidney's theory is closer to Gosson's theory even than this. It has not merely the same bases but also the same form. I have underlined the sentence from Sidney,

Our erected wit maketh us know what perfectiŏ is, and yet our infected wil keepeth us frŏ reaching unto it.

But this is the very model of Gosson's theory. Gosson grants that the mind of the poet, his soul, whatever we take to be his erected wit, has before it an ideal. But the poem is not written or read through this erected wit. A poem is made, and is moving, through the senses. The senses make it pleasing, they make it worldly, they infect it as they infect the will of man. So Gosson understands poetry; and so, we now see, Sidney understands it. And so Gosson and Sidney understand man himself, who houses both an erected wit and the infection of his senses: who in his mind can make 'an other nature', and is yet bound to the nature which his senses know. To Sidney, as to Gosson, the poem is only the shadow of an ideal poetry: a shadow cast through the senses.

Here we have reached the true quarrel between Gosson and Sidney. Both think that poetry is an ideal good; both think that poems abuse this good.

For Gosson, the abuse outweighs the good. He can show how full of abuses are actual poems, and how they are used for ill. If there were no source of ideal good which is free from abuse, then no doubt men would have to use poems as a source of good: an infected source, 'nor to be read at any time without good caution'. But for Gosson there is a source of good free from the abuse of the senses: the bible. The bible was written, at the least was directly inspired, by God. No poet has damaged its good by writing it through the senses. It can be read and loved without the pleasure of the senses: so the Puritans claimed, and in proof stripped worship of everything which could be thought to please the senses. Thus God speaks to us through the prophets directly; he speaks to us through poets only by way of the abusing senses. To claim as Sidney does that he speaks through poets almost as he speaks through prophets, is to hide in the word 'almost' just that fever of the senses which the Puritans fought.

This is Gosson's side of the quarrel. For Sidney, the ideal good outweighs its abuses. It must needs do so, if there are to be ideals at all; because Sidney will not allow that any ideal can be freed wholly from the abuse of the senses. Man cannot act except through the senses. Whatever is spoken or written is so through the senses, and in turn moves others through the senses. The prophets were inspired; but what they wrote was revealed to them in no way which could leave their senses wholly out of the writing. Thus their inspiration was not different in kind from the inspiration of poets; and God does speak through poets, almost as he speaks through prophets. We see again why Sidney, however lamely, claims the bible as poetry. He is claiming that men are moved by the bible as they are moved by poems, through the senses. Even worship cannot be stripped, as the Puritans sought to strip it, of all that pleases the senses. The ideal good can reach man only through his senses. In doing so, the ideal is damaged; but man must make the most of the ideal and the least of the damage. The ideal good outweighs the damage, because we must make it outweigh it; for only so can we see the ideal, however clouded:

Everie understanding, knoweth the skill of ech Artificer standeth in that *Idea*, or fore conceit of the worke, and not in the worke it selfe. And that the Poet hath that *Idea*, is manifest.

The work itself cannot be free from the infected will; it is the business of the erected wit to look behind it in order to 'know what perfectiõ is'.

We see that Sidney's theory of poetry and Gosson's are the same. Both think that poetry is an ideal good; both think that poems abuse this good. Their quarrel is, whether the abuse outweighs the good, or whether the good outweighs the abuse. It hangs on the question, whether man can know any ideal except through the abusing senses. Sidney holds that he cannot. This claim neatly turns the tables on Gosson. Gosson had charged Sidney to point to that *Phœnix* in *Arabia*, a poem without abuses. Now it is Gosson who, to meet Sidney's charge, must find a *Phœnix* in *Arabia*: a book in which an ideal is set out free from the infection of the senses. Gosson points to the bible. But it is not a telling example. Even of those who think that the bible is inspired, few are willing to read it in the Puritan way, stripped of the pleasure of the senses. The greatest body of those who think it inspired, the Roman Catholic Church, says of it what Milton said of the *Arcadia*: that it is 'not to be read at any time without good caution'. Most of us do not think that the bible is inspired. We often praise it for its sounding prose, or a like pleasure of the senses. We must grant Sidney's claim, that there is no work in which the erected wit is free from the infected will; and that therefore poems cannot be damned, for being so infected.

3

I have set out the principle which Sidney and Gosson shared in their theories of poetry, and the principle on which they quarrelled. In the quarrel, I think Sidney was right; and we must think him right, unless like Gosson we are strictly Puritan. Only the Puritan will deny Sidney's claim, that no ideal can be written of in a way which is free from the infection of the senses. Nor is there force in the Puritan answer that the bible is written in such a way. For the bible is then not the work of man; and poems may still claim a place higher than other works of man. Sidney gave a list of the sciences, and claimed that the knowledge of nature which they give stands below the knowledge of 'an other nature' which poetry shadows. This claim is not rebutted by the Puritan example of the bible. If that example damns poetry, it damns all man's knowledge.

Only for one reason can the Puritan example be taken to damn poetry more surely than it damns worldly knowledge: because poetry makes higher claims than the worldly knowledges. Astronomy, or history, is frankly worldly. Because it knows its narrow bounds, it can be allowed within them on sufferance in the Puritan world; it is useful there, and no more. Poetry can claim no such usefulness. We have seen how helpless Sidney is in face of Gosson's charges that, in the worldly meaning, poetry 'dwelleth longest in those pointes, that profite least'. If poetry is to claim a place, it must claim it on unworldly grounds; and base it not in nature but in 'an other nature'. For this claim the Puritan will damn it. Yet Gosson did not wholly deny this claim. He did allow an ideal of poetry. He damned poetry only because it damaged its ideal and made it worldly. In Gosson's thought there is a place both for the ideal and for the worldly. There is no place for a mongrel of the two. Gosson has this answer to Sidney's claims: that to Sidney poetry is both ideal and worldly, and that these two views are contradictory.

We cannot deny that there is such a contradiction. We have seen it in Sidney's pains to answer Gosson's charges not once but twice: not only from his un-worldly principle, but also with worldly answers.

We see it again in his pains to add to his own theory of poetry a second theory, 'a more ordinarie opening'. This is Aristotle's theory, that '*Poesie* is an Art of *Imitation*'. It is not of a piece with Sidney's theory. Indeed, if the Imitation in Aristotle's theory is imitation of nature, then plainly the theory contradicts Sidney's theory. Sidney shields himself from the contradiction by saying that it is not the known nature which poets imitate. No; the best poets

to imitate, borrow nothing of what is, hath bin, or shall be, but range onely reined with learned discretion, into the divine consideration of what may be and should be.

This is not a happy flight from the contradiction. It tells us that the poet does not imitate the known nature; it does not tell us what he does imitate. Clearly the word Imitation is out of place in this account. It is rather the word Making in his own theory which Sidney is unravelling. He leaves untouched the contradiction between making and imitating: between poetry thought of as an ideal, and poetry as a patterning. And his awkward gloss sharpens the contradiction. For he must now ask to what end poets imitate; he must answer,

These indeed do meerly make to imitate, and imitate both to delight & teach, and delight to move men to take that goodnesse in hand, which without delight they would flie as from a stranger; and teach to make them know that goodnesse wherunto they are moved.

This is surely counter to Sidney's theory. That theory claims that poetry is an ideal; it does not claim that poetry has a use in the social, natural world. And I have shown how ill Sidney could hold against Gosson that poetry does have a social use. Now Sidney again seeks to give poetry such a use. Its use is to teach. If this is indeed a social use, it cannot withstand Gosson's charges. Gosson could show in the poems of his time that what poetry teaches is fruitless and wanton. If the knowledge to be got from poems is worldly knowledge, then without doubt it is bad. And Sidney says that poems teach us this knowledge by delighting us. Thus poems have a use only because they give pleasure. Not the ideal of poems but its sensuous dress makes them useful. Gosson has cried out against this pleasure of the senses; Sidney himself has belittled it, and has given it a place only because no ideal can be free from it. Now Sidney seems to forget his theory, and to go back to the hopeless claim that poems are useful because they please.

We should see how unhappily Sidney has slipped back to this claim. He has done so for the sake of a theory with which he has nothing in common, and which he has hardly taken pains to understand. In trying to give meaning to Aristotle's theory, Sidney has snatched at the acts 'to delight & teach': they are to give the noblest meaning of 'to imitate'. This is not a deep reading of Aristotle, and Sidney took it from others too readily. We might therefore discount the awkward passage. We should gain nothing by discounting it. It is true that the passage is out of place in Sidney's theory. But the contradiction

which it marks is not out of place. The contradiction
must be understood and met.

The contradiction is between Sidney's belief that
poetry is an ideal, and his claim that it has a worldly
use, to teach. To understand it we must therefore
understand what Sidney means by the word, to teach:
what knowledge he thinks worthy to be taught. We
have come back to the question which I have asked:
What does Sidney mean by knowledge? Now Sidney
answers vaguely that the knowledge which poems
teach is Goodness. The word is as puzzling as ever.
Does Goodness mean the good; the ideal of poetry?
Or does it mean good conduct; that which is socially
right?

Such two-edged words as Goodness are the keys
to Sidney's and to Renaissance thought. The knowledge for which they stand is certainly not worldly
knowledge, as astronomy and history are worldly
knowledges. Yet it is a knowledge, Sidney believes,
which can rule the worldly knowledges. Once again
Sidney makes a list of the sciences; and asks which is
the best source of this knowledge. He finds that two
are best.

The *Philosopher* therefore, and the *Historian*, are they
which would win the goale, the one by precept, the other
by example: but both, not having both, doo both halt.

And having shown that in poems there is both the
'generall notion' of philosophy and the 'particuler
example' of history, he can say proudly:

I thinke it may be manifest, that the *Poet* with that
same hand of delight, doth draw the mind more effec-

tually then any other Art doth. And so a conclusion not unfitly ensue, that as vertue is the most excellēt resting place for al worldly learning to make his end of, so *Poetry*, being the most familiar to teach it, and most Princely to move towards it, in the most excellent worke, is the most excellent workeman.

Like the word Goodness, Virtue is a two-edged word; and is a key to Sidney's thought. Unlike Goodness, it is not a vague word to Sidney and his friends. Virtue is the pass-word to the group of men whose centre was Sidney's sister Mary, Countess of Pembroke. When one of these men, Edmund Spenser, printed his poem *The Faerie Queene*, he printed with it a letter to say that the end of the poem is to teach virtue; and he gave examples of the virtues which he had in mind.

In that Faery Queene I meane glory in my generall intention.

So in the person of Prince Arthure I sette forth magnificence in particular, which vertue for that (according to Aristotle and the rest) it is the perfection of all the rest, and conteineth in it them all, therefore in the whole course I mention the deedes of Arthure applyable to that vertue.

This is enlightening. Whatever we may think are the social virtues, we do not think that Glory is one of them. Magnificence is the Renaissance translation of Aristotle's μεγαλοψυχία, greatness of soul. Whether we give it this or its common meaning, magnificence is not a social virtue. No commonwealth claims these as virtues of citizenship and worldly conduct. To Spenser and his friends, therefore, virtue does not mean a worldly good. But it is not easy to fix the good which it does mean. William Blake wrote angrily in the margin of Bacon's *Essays*,

What do these knaves mean by virtue? Do they mean war and its horrors, and its heroic villains?

The charge is just. The Renaissance writers would not forget the classical meaning of virtue: bravery. They hankered after acts like Sidney's death, of gallant glory and magnificence: and they would not face the evil extravagance, the lust for glory of heroic villains, which these acts breed. Blake wrote aptly,

> The Strongest Poison ever known
> Came from Caesar's Laurel Crown.
> Nought can deform the Human Race
> Like to the Armour's iron brace.

The couplets sum the evil which the ambitions of glory and magnificence may draw upon each man and upon the commonwealth.

Blake's reading of the word Virtue has a model in Sidney. In one of the sonnets of *Astrophel and Stella*, Sidney writes,

> I do not envie *Aristotles* wit,
> Nor do aspire to *Cæsars* bleeding fame;
> But that which once may win thy cruell hart:
> Thou art my Wit, and thou my Vertue art.

Here the careful verse certainly couples Virtue with *Cæsar's* bleeding fame, the fame which Caesar won in war. This is the classical meaning, with which Blake taxed these writers. I set it by the side of Gosson's regret that the English are no longer warlike.

Gallants and Puritans alike at times read virtue literally, as the heroics of war. For the virtues of which they write are not social virtues. Indeed, Sidney does not write of virtues: he writes of virtue as a whole, which is not to be split into this and that social gift. To the minds of these writers virtue is an ideal. It is set against the infected will of the senses. Sidney writes,

> So while thy beautie drawes the heart to love,
> As fast thy Vertue bends that love to good:
> But ah, Desire still cries, give me some food;

and the pathos of this underlines that virtue is set against the desire of the senses. There is a hint here that virtue can be read in its commonplace meaning, as chastity; and the hint recalls how two-edged is the word, and Sidney's thought behind it. Sidney is packing into the one word a state of mind which is complex; and which is the model of the Renaissance thought. The three lines I have quoted show the threads of this ravelled thought. In them, virtue denies that which desire cries for; thus virtue brings with it chastity. But it merely brings chastity: it is not itself chastity. Chastity stands to Virtue, the verse implies, exactly as Desire stands to Love. Desire and chastity are kinds of conduct; love and virtue are ideals, which prompt conduct, but which are far greater than the sum of conduct which can be drawn from them. This is the Renaissance plea to live both in the world and the ideal; the Renaissance search to hold together, almost by force, the contradiction between the actual and the ideal. For Sidney, neither the actual nor the ideal stands quite alone. There is some shadow of the ideal Virtue in the actual world: a virtue of conduct, called chastity. And there is a shadow of desire in the ideal: an idealised desire called love. This thought makes the logic of such a sonnet as that in which Stella tells Sidney

> That love she did, but loved a Love not blind,
> Which would not let me, whom she loved, decline
> From nobler course, fit for my birth and mind:
> And therefore, by her Loves authority,
> Wild me these tempests of vaine love to flie,
> And anchor fast my selfe on *Vertues* shore.
> Alas, if this the only mettall be
> Of *Love*, new-coind to helpe my beggery,
> Deare, love me not, that ye may love me more.

Under this thought, the word Love has become as double-edged as the word Virtue. Its two meanings make the whole force of the sonnet. There is no play of meanings; the two meanings are set baldly one against the other. Stella is speaking of love as an ideal; the Sidney within the sonnet is asking for love, the bodily desire. The link between them is Stella herself, who can call up the two opposing states of mind. This is the clearest account which Sidney gives of his belief that every thought on each of the two sides, the ideal and the actual, has its counterpart on the other; and that in this way the two are linked.

This belief is of a piece with the belief of Sidney's which I have stressed: that no ideal can be wholly freed from the infection of the senses. Sidney was then thinking of the ideal only as set down in speech or writing. Now he enlarges that belief; and holds that

the ideal must always have a part in the world of
the senses. As he sees it, the ideal cannot be freed
from the thought of the man who has it in mind. It
is therefore bound by that thought, and by the
thinker's senses through his thought. If we unravel
it we get two strands: the abstract ideal, and the
shadow of the ideal in the senses. But we cannot
hold either strand alone in the mind. And in the
same way, Sidney believes, worldly thought is also
made of two strands: the senses, and a shadow of the
senses in the ideal. At each stage, the ideal and the
senses are linked. The linking force is the mind itself.
In Sidney's poems, the linking force is the model of
the best mind, Stella. Sidney writes of it clearly.

> Soules joy, bend not those morning starres from me,
> Where Vertue is made strong by Beauties might,
> Where *Love* is chastnesse, Paine doth learne delight,
> And Humblenesse growes one with Majestie.

Here the link is in those morning stars, Stella's
eyes, which are the symbol of the mind. They link
the ideal to worldly sense or conduct; and we can
read this even in the last line, if we recall Spenser's
virtues, glory and magnificence.

Sidney's Elizabethan Virtue therefore plays a
double part. It is such an ideal as Gosson could hold,
and which Spenser could think truly summed in the
word Magnificence. And at the same time it has its
shadow in the simple virtues of conduct: chasteness,
humbleness, or bodily love. To Gosson there was no
such shadow; conduct could not be linked to the
ideal, except in the set way in which the Ten Com-

mandments are linked to God. But to Sidney and
his sister's Renaissance friends, the link could be
made. The mind at its best, fine feeling, a great
passion might make it. For it could only be made
at such times, when man reaches out of himself.
We now understand why the virtuous conduct of
the Elizabethans was always extravagant conduct:
the worship of Elizabeth as the model of magnificence,
the search for El Dorado, the hope for '*Cæsars* bleeding
fame'. For the ideal virtues have a social use only
in times of social extravagance. Only then, in war
and discovery, do the wild virtues of Drake, Grenville,
of Sidney himself, earn a place in society. Blake is
right: to the Elizabethans, virtue often did mean
'war and its horrors, and its heroic villains'. And
Gosson was as much infected with this meaning as
was Sidney. It is a false meaning. The ideal virtue
cannot simply be carried into conduct: that gives
only the tawdry magnificence of Elizabeth, and the
wasted glory of Sidney's death. If, as Sidney believed,
it can be made to shape conduct, it must do so
through fine mind and passion. The place of these is
not taken by Elizabeth's cunning and the hysteria of
war.

Sidney more than another Elizabethan proved his
belief. He did learn to hold the ideal virtue, and
to pass it through the linking mind and passion so
that it became a true guide to conduct. The story of
how he learnt it is *Astrophel and Stella*. There Stella,
the symbol of the best mind in passion, step by step
makes virtue the master of conduct.

Oft with true sighes, oft with uncalled teares,
Now with slow words, now with dumbe eloquence
I *Stellas* eyes assaid, invade her eares;
But this at last is her sweet breath'd defence:
That who indeed infelt affection beares,
So captives to his Saint both soule and sence,
That wholly hers, all selfnesse he forbeares,
Then his desires he learnes, his lives course thence.

Sidney is stressing that there is a force to bind soule
and sence and desire: the ideal force of Stella, the
'vertuous Soule'. Sidney has seen it change him. He
has written,

Stella, whence doth this new assault arise,
A conquerd yolden ransackt heart to winne?
That not my soule, which at thy foot did fall,
Long since forc'd by thy beames, but stone nor tree
By Sences priviledge, can scape from thee.

The change is followed step by step. First the soul
was Stella's proper range; now the soulless things,
symbols of the world of the senses, have fallen under
her power. Again the symbol is the eyes, symbol of
mind; and its working is in the heart, symbol of
passion. It was this change which, to Sidney, was
'teaching', and whose knowledge was virtue. It is
nowhere set out more seriously than in *Astrophel and
Stella*.

4

I have followed Sidney's account of poetry through
three stages. At the one stage, Sidney is merely
meeting Gosson's charges, that poetry by its nature
breeds abuses and overthrows virtue; and striking

at them with any weapon to hand. He is trying to show that poems have worldly uses as well as abuses, and may lead the reader to virtuous conduct as well as vicious conduct. In this Sidney fails. Poetry cannot claim to have a worldly use. It upholds no social right. If it has a right use, then it is such a right use as Gosson allows it: an ideal use, which in actual poems is needs overborne by the abuse of the senses. Here Gosson is right, and Sidney wrong.

And at the second stage, Sidney allows that Gosson is right. He sets out his own theory of poetry, and it is exactly Gosson's theory. Like Gosson, Sidney knows poetry as an ideal. In the writing of poems, this ideal falls under the infection of the senses, and is damaged. To Gosson, the damage outweighs the ideal good. But to Sidney, no ideal can be wholly freed from this damage. We must read the ideal of poetry as best we can through the damage, because we can never read an ideal in any other way.

At the third stage, Sidney carries this belief a step farther. However purely we try to think of the ideal, we cannot unravel the thought from the senses. The ideal has a shadow in the world of the senses; the senses have shadows in the ideal. In the mind of man, and in his best feelings and passions, these two are linked; and then the ideal can shape the conduct of man, at times and at his best. At those times, man wins an instant knowledge of the ideal, which is the only knowledge worth having. It is the knowledge of Virtue.

Virtue, the two-edged word, is the key to Sidney's

thought in this. It is the rare link of two fields. On the one side is the world we know: the world of the senses, of social good, of man and manly thinking; the world which to Sidney was nature. On the other side is the ideal, the field of absolute good, of the soul, of that which is more than man and which is set against nature; that which Sidney said the poet makes, 'an other nature'. Sidney and Gosson are at one that the poet sees this other nature, and writes of it as best he can through the known nature. To Gosson, this is the unforgivable ruin of the other nature, which comes to the end of the poem damaged, bedraggled, and vicious. And Gosson can point to the poems of his time to show that he sees truly. Nevertheless Sidney will not believe him. To Sidney, the poet is setting out the ideal in the only way in which it can be set out. Certainly the poet's failures are frightful. But Sidney's faith is not to be put down. Almost childishly he holds to this:

Yet shall it be so farre from concluding, that the abuse should give reproach to the abused, that cõtrariwise, it is a good reason, that whatsoever being abused, doth most harme, being rightly used (and upon the right use, ech thing receives his title) doth most good.

In the moments when the poet does not fail, the ideal 'other nature' works through him and shapes the nature of man. In those moments man learns Virtue. Nowhere else can he learn it, and no other knowledge is worth learning.

And so a conclusion not unfitly ensue, that as vertue is the most excellẽt resting place for al worldly learning to make his end of, so *Poetry*, being the most familiar to teach it, and most Princely to move towards it, in the most excellent worke, is the most excellent workeman.

The faith is almost childish; and Sidney knew hardly any poems to uphold it. Yet Sidney held to the faith. Sidney was dead before his friend Spenser, with the same faith held in the same word Virtue, wrote *The Faerie Queene*. He was dead before Ben Jonson, Shakespeare, Donne, Milton, Dryden, Pope, Gray, Blake, Wordsworth, Coleridge wrote. In them, Sidney's faith came true. Only because we have their poems can we be so sure that Gosson was wrong when he held that poetry needs 'dwelleth longest in those pointes, that profite least'. And we owe their poems to such faith as Sidney's.

For Sidney's faith was that poetry can be serious: that in it the poet's self can speak, to itself. *Astrophel and Stella* is the story of the making of Sidney's self. And it was from *Astrophel and Stella* that I described the faith which Sidney summed in the word Virtue. We shall not understand Sidney's meaning in that word better than by taking as its symbol and name Stella herself: who links soul and desire, and through whom Sidney learns that the ideal can shape conduct. Sidney has learnt Virtue, and Stella is its symbol. *Astrophel and Stella* is the symbol of the learning. It gives meaning to Sidney's faith. I have come back to the sentence which I stressed first: that *Astrophel and Stella* is a serious poem, and that from it the *Defence of Poesie* takes meaning.

PERCY BYSSHE SHELLEY

I

IT IS apt to couple Shelley's name with Sidney's. Sidney believed that poetry moves men to Virtue, away from their worldly ends. We think that this is like Shelley's belief. Surely when Shelley set out his belief in the *Defence of Poetry* he did so with Sidney's *Defence* as his model?

Shelley did take Sidney's *Defence of Poesie* for his model. He did find what he thought a likeness between Sidney's belief and his own. Shelley's readers have been willing to find the same likeness. They have called Shelley an idealist. He spoke so often of higher ends, his plans for good were so vague and his zeal was so general, that it has seemed plain to them that he could not be called a materialist. It is not my point to call him the one or the other. But it is to the point to recall that pity and hope for man do not make an ideal. Shelley had kind and fine feelings. He wished to spare men pain, to make them happy, to better their taste: to set free all the good which he saw shut up in them. We should not belittle this passionate good-will. But we must not mistake it for such an ideal as I have traced in Sidney. The evils which Shelley saw were social evils. Men were not good because they were poor and enslaved. Make them rich and free, and the good in them will be set free. This is a worthy belief; but it is not Sidney's belief. Sidney did believe that men must be rich and free before they can be good. He did not believe that they need be nothing else, to be good. He believed that men must seek Virtue at all times. This is the world of difference between Sidney and Shelley, between the Renaissance and the Romantic Revival, which I wish to set out.

Like Sidney's, Shelley's *Defence* is to answer a striking attack. The attack is Thomas Love Peacock's *Four Ages of Poetry*. Unlike Gosson, Peacock does not believe that poetry is evil in itself. He believes that poetry has a place in some societies; but none in others. It merely happens, says Peacock, that poetry has no place in his own society. Peacock believes that there are four kinds or ages of society; and that poetry has a place in only two of them. It has a place in the lawless iron age: then it flatters and guides the fighting, plundering chiefs. And it has a place in the golden age, when the plundering men are first held by laws, and when they look back with awe to their fathers who won kingdoms. Then it enlarges this awe to make a tradition. In both ages, poetry holds and hands on what knowledge there is: to do this is truly its place.

But it holds this place only so long as it holds the only knowledge. When, in the silver age, society at last learns to reason, poetry fails before the new knowledge. A few poets try to reason in verse; they are outdone by the reasoners in prose. A few copy the poems of the golden age; but their refined verse has no meaning for their society. And the poets themselves

come to see this. They see that they are not reasoners.
They see how dead is their refinement. Wildly they
try to go back to the golden age. They write about
nature, about simple people and savages; they set
themselves against the speech and the manners of
their age. But the new age which they make is only
an age of brass. For they have lost their place in
society. Society is now wholly fixed upon reason.
It has outgrown the tradition which gave life to
poetry in the golden age, and the unreasoned feelings
proper to it. To go back to these is to go against the
growth of society. 'This is the second childhood of
poetry', writes Peacock; and 'A poet in our times
is a semi-barbarian in a civilized community'.

For the brass age is Peacock's own age. The poets
who write about nature, simpletons, and savages, are
the Lake poets. Peacock makes fun of them in passages
which are delightful and well known. But more to
the point are the passages in which Peacock sets
against one another the claims of reason and of
poetry.

Feeling and passion are best painted in, and roused by,
ornamental and figurative language; but the reason and
the understanding are best addressed in the simplest
and most unvarnished phrase. Pure reason and dispassionate truth would be perfectly ridiculous in verse,
as we may judge by versifying one of Euclid's demon-
strations. This will be found true of all dispassionate
reasoning whatever, and all reasoning that requires comprehensive views and enlarged combinations. It is only
the more tangible points of morality, those which com-
mand assent at once, those which have a mirror in every
mind, and in which the severity of reason is warmed and

rendered palatable by being mixed up with feeling and imagination, that are applicable even to what is called moral poetry: and as the sciences of morals and of mind advance towards perfection, as they become more enlarged and comprehensive in their views, as reason gains the ascendancy in them over imagination and feeling, poetry can no longer accompany them in their progress, but drops into the back ground, and leaves them to advance alone.

This is remarkable writing. It goes on smoothly, with a pomp which is engaging. But it is full of tricks: false logic, false couplings, and false likenesses. Peacock is hurrying his argument beyond its scope; and is aware of it. He can show that reasoning is done more freely in prose than in verse. He can show that his society reasons more often than other societies. He is therefore right to say that verse is less useful to his society than it has been to other societies. But Peacock wants to say more than this. He wants to say that his society is better than other societies. He wants to say that therefore verse is less useful as society grows better; that those needs which verse serves are childish; and that this is true not only of society but of each man alone. He wants to claim reason as the only good of the mind. The tricks of the passage are to stake this claim. They take it as a matter of course that truth is found only by reasoning; that the mind grows fuller and more understanding only as it reasons more; and that what knowledge the mind has otherwise, if it is not false, is trifling. Peacock is stretching the word Reason to a new meaning. He has used it to mean logical reasoning; and has shown that this is out of place in verse, because it can be done better in prose. Verse should be used to do only what it does better than prose; and Peacock has told us what that is:

Feeling and passion are best painted in, and roused by, ornamental and figurative language.

Now Peacock tries to make reason mean the truth. But have not feeling and passion a part in truth, as surely as has reasoning? Peacock shirks this question skilfully. He speaks of 'dispassionate truth'; he couples this with the phrase 'pure reason'; and when then he speaks of 'dispassionate reasoning', the reader cannot doubt that he means pure truth. For a moment, Peacock is making of reasoning an ideal; it is the whole reason of man, and at last the truth itself.

Peacock does not make this claim again; for it is not in keeping with his thought. It is forced on him here by the argument which he is using: that because poetry does not reason well, it cannot tell the truth. Only to this end does he enlarge reason to the standing of an ideal truth; and claim that it has a worth to each man other than its social use. When he next sets reason against poetry, he has moved back to his own ground.

The philosophic mental tranquillity which looks round with an equal eye on all external things, collects a store of ideas, discriminates their relative value, assigns to all their proper place, and from the materials of useful knowledge thus collected, appreciated, and arranged, forms new combinations that impress the stamp of their power

and utility on the real business of life, is diametrically
the reverse of that frame of mind which poetry inspires,
or from which poetry can emanate. The highest inspirations of poetry are resolvable into three ingredients: the
rant of unregulated passion, the whining of exaggerated
feeling, and the cant of factitious sentiment: and can
therefore serve only to ripen a splendid lunatic like
Alexander, a puling driveller like Werter, or a morbid
dreamer like Wordsworth. It can never make a philosopher, nor a statesman, nor in any class of life an useful
or rational man.

The form is unchanged: again we are told that poetry
is fit only for passion and feeling, that these are
trifling things, and that the greater worth is reason.
But the charge itself is changed. Peacock no longer
speaks of the ideal 'dispassionate truth' with which
he had flirted for a moment. Reason is no longer his
word like a flag, to rally all the powers of light.
Peacock remembers it only once in the passage, in
the humble coupling 'an useful or rational man'.
Where it stood we have the grey phrase 'philosophic
mental tranquillity'. The phrase owes something to
Wordsworth; yet it is the test by which Wordsworth
is to be proved a ranting and over-feeling poet. Again
we are aware that Peacock is confused and ill at ease
in his argument. What he wants to say is simple:
that in England in 1820 poetry has no social uses.
This claim cannot be challenged. We have seen how
hopelessly Sidney failed in challenging a like claim
in 1580. But Peacock is still trying to press his claim
farther. He is trying to claim that there are no uses
other than social uses. Therefore he enlarges the

social virtues of his time so that they shall seem to be
the only virtues. Peacock has summed the social
virtues of his time in the word Reason. Since he cannot
uphold his claim that reason is the whole of virtue,
Peacock changes his ground subtly. He no longer
sets reason against poetry. He now sets against one
another the frames of mind in which men reason
and in which they write poems. The highest good
is philosophic mental tranquillity, in which men
can collect, appreciate, arrange and form new
combinations of useful knowledge; and this is the
frame of mind in which men reason. Against this
frame and these means is set the frame of mind in
which poems are written. But Peacock does not tell
us what this frame is. With happy sleight, he speaks
all at once of the 'inspirations' of poetry; and hides
the trick in a burst of rant against unregulated
passion, exaggerated feeling, and factitious sentiment. Peacock is confusing the mood in which a
poem is written with the habit of mind of poets; and
both, with the ends which the poem can serve. A poem
may be written in an orderly or a disorderly mood:
and either of these may be the mood of an orderly
or a disorderly mind: either may move a reader either
to orderly or to disorderly thinking. Thus the instant
mood put into or drawn from the poem may have
a use for an orderly mind as well as for a disorderly
mind. The use for which Peacock hankers, to make
an useful or rational man, certainly cannot lie in
this mood.

Can it lie in the habits of thought by which Peacock's

society set store? Peacock describes the scientific
habit which his age was learning; and he tries to
prove its worth for all ages, by claiming that it is
the only orderly habit of thought. All thinking which
does not collect, appreciate, arrange, is disorderly
thinking, and therefore worthless: this is Peacock's
claim. It is to uphold this claim that Peacock con-
fuses the mood in which a poem is written with the
poetic habits of thought. The confusion is part of
the confusion between the means of thinking and
the end of thinking on which Peacock's claim is built.
The scientific habit of thought, which collects, appreciates, arranges, is a means. Wordsworth showed that
it can be a means even to poetic ends. It is not the
only orderly habit of thought; because the order of
thinking is shaped by its end: and therefore only
thinking whose end is scientific is bound to the
scientific order. Thinking whose end is poetic has its
own order: it need not be disorderly. So the thought
which lies in a couplet which I have quoted from
Blake,

> The Strongest Poison ever known
> Came from Caesar's Laurel Crown,

and the thought which is harsh in Sidney's lines,

> So while thy beautie drawes the heart to love,
> As fast thy Vertue bends that love to good:
> But ah, Desire still cries, give me some food,

are orderly thoughts; although their order is not that
which collects, appreciates, arranges.

No way of thinking is orderly in itself, and worthy in itself. Scientific thinking, and all thinking, is orderly only in being fitted to its end. It is worthy only as the end which it serves, and which gives it order, is worthy. And Peacock himself understands this. He does not describe the scientific habit without pointing to its end. The scientific habit of thought not merely

collects a store of ideas, discriminates their relative value, assigns to all their proper place.

No; its virtue is to go a step further: that it,

from the materials of useful knowledge thus collected, appreciated, and arranged, forms new combinations that impress the stamp of their power and utility on the real business of life.

Peacock is careful still to leave the act vague. He is describing a philosophic mental tranquillity; and is shy of telling us that its end is to make governments and engines. The end is therefore still called genteelly the real business of life. What is this business? It is what poetry cannot do; and Peacock must at last tell us what that is without mincing. Poetry

can never make a philosopher, nor a statesman, nor in any class of life an useful or rational man. It cannot claim the slightest share in any one of the comforts and utilities of life of which we have witnessed so many and so rapid advances.

The end of scientific thinking is to make an useful or rational man. This is to serve the real business of life; and that coy phrase is at last unmasked as 'the comforts and utilities of life'.

I have followed Peacock closely to this point, because I have wanted to leave no doubt that this and only this is his charge. *The Four Ages of Poetry* is an entertaining and skittish piece of writing; and it is not easy to know how seriously to take any part of it. Shelley, taking it very seriously, makes his answers look owlish. Since then, readers who have been afraid to be thought as humourless as Shelley have read *The Four Ages of Poetry* as a piece of sprightliness and no more. Of the two, Shelley's is the better reading. No doubt Peacock was having his fun, and no doubt Shelley failed to see it. But the points which Peacock makes, in fun or in earnest, are serious points. And in choosing to write only half-seriously, Peacock has not been quite artless. The banter, the pomp, and the rant, hide a shuffling in argument which would not pass in a serious attack. Peacock knows that in the end he has only one charge: that poetry is not useful to the society of his time. To strengthen this charge, he has tried to show that this society is itself worthy. It is a society built on reasoned, scientific thinking; and Peacock has therefore tried to make the reader grant that this is the best kind of thinking. He has tried to do this in two ways. First, he has tried to hurry the reader into taking Reason to be the same as Truth. Second, he has tried to show that scientific thinking is the only orderly thinking. Peacock has argued neither of these claims; and has hidden the lack of argument in banter. I have taken both claims seriously, and shown that both claims fail. There is left only the simple charge, which Peacock tried so hard to strengthen: the charge that poetry is not socially useful.

It cannot claim the slightest share in any one of the comforts and utilities of life of which we have witnessed so many and so rapid advances.

This is a charge which Shelley should not have denied.

2

Shelley understands Peacock's case very well. *The Defence of Poetry* at once goes to the base of Peacock's charges: the scope of reason. I quote its first sentence.

According to one mode of regarding those two classes of mental action, which are called reason and imagination, the former may be considered as mind contemplating the relations borne by one thought to another, however produced; and the latter, as mind acting upon those thoughts so as to colour them with its own light, and composing from them as from elements, other thoughts, each containing within itself the principle of its own integrity.

The force of this is plain. Shelley is setting out to deny Peacock's claim that reason is the only good of the mind. To do so, he praises another act of the mind: imagination. The word is new to us; but others than Shelley had used it since the word Invention had gone out with the Augustans. Blake and Coleridge used it. Like Shelley, they set it against a mechanical gift: against reason, against the fancy. Like Shelley, they were putting right a one-sided picture of the world. For Shelley is showing that Peacock's is a one-sided picture. Reason does not tell the whole truth. Neither, of course, does imagination: Shelley need only show that imagination is part of the truth. Unhappily, Shelley is not content to show this. He feels that he must show more. He feels that he must claim that imagination is the greater act of the mind. It tells more of the truth. Reason is merely its tool,

Reason is to imagination as the instrument to the agent, as the body to the spirit, as the shadow to the substance.

What ground has Shelley for this claim? What is the imagination for which he makes it?

The answer begins oddly.

A child at play by itself will express its delight by its voice and motions; and every inflexion of tone and gesture will bear exact relation to a corresponding antitype in the pleasurable impressions which awakened it; it will be the reflected image of that impression; and as the lyre trembles and sounds after the wind has died away, so the child seeks, by prolonging in its voice and motions the duration of the effect, to prolong also a consciousness of the cause. In relation to the objects which delight a child, these expressions are what poetry is to higher objects.

This act is the model of the imagination. The child or poet first draws pleasure from things outside itself. He wishes to make the pleasure lasting: to do so, he gives it form in speech or act. The child in pleasure chuckles, shall we say; and then finds that if he goes on chuckling, he goes on feeling pleasure. This

machinery is the imagination. Its form is given by
the child's or poet's pleasure, and through it by the
things which gave pleasure. And its end is to make
this pleasure lasting.

This machine, which Shelley describes, certainly
has a place in the mind. The question is, Does it
make poems? And the answer is plainly, It does not.
We may believe that the need to write a poem arises
in the poet by means of this machine. We may believe
that the child chuckles and the poet writes in order
to make his pleasure lasting. And we may be ready,
like Coleridge, to stretch the meaning of Pleasure as
wide as this belief asks. But we cannot believe that
Shelley has told us how poems are made: how the
child or the poet chooses that act which he thinks
apt to his pleasure. He has told us that there is
a well fixed scale of such acts:

every inflexion of tone and gesture will bear exact
relation to a corresponding antitype in the pleasurable
impressions which awakened it.

But it is this scale for which we ask, and which we
are not given. Without this scale, Shelley's theory of
the imagination tells us at most why poets write.
What we ask of such a theory is to tell us why poets
write as they do.

Shelley's machine is at most a first step to the
imagination; and we may ask why Shelley troubles
himself with it. He does so under the press of Peacock's
charges. Peacock has set up reason as the good of
man, and as his ever growing need. In setting up
imagination as a rival good, Shelley is therefore at

pains to prove that it is an everlasting need of man. Peacock has said that poems meet no need of the men of his time. Shelley is saying that poems are 'the expression of the imagination', and that imagination meets a need of men at all times. It is the need to make their pleasure known and to make it lasting. Shelley's machine shows how men meet this need. Shelley may have told us only what prompts the poet to write. Nevertheless he can claim that the prompting reaches all men, and acts in Peacock's age as it did in the golden age.

But Shelley's example does not prove even this. Peacock might grant that

a child at play by itself will express its delight by its voice and motions.

He might grant Shelley's artless corollary,

The savage (for the savage is to ages what the child is to years) expresses the emotions produced in him by surrounding objects in a similar manner; and language and gesture, together with plastic or pictorial imitation, become the image of the combined effect of those objects and his apprehension of them.

For these merely bear out Peacock's claim that those needs which poems meet are childish and savage needs. Peacock did not deny that there were such needs. He saw them as the needs of the feelings and the passions; and he held that all but children and savages should be able to master these needs. Shelley has called them the needs of the imagination; but nothing in his theory sets them above the needs which Peacock knew and thought unworthy.

Shelley must therefore go on to show that men in society feel the same needs; and that the needs are apt to their new state. The child and the savage had been moved by the objects of nature. Now, says Shelley,

man in society, with all his passions and his pleasures, next becomes the object of the passions and pleasures of man; an additional class of emotions produces an augmented treasure of expression.

Shelley is claiming that there are other pleasures which are social. The need which man feels to make these pleasures known and lasting could not have been felt outside society. It must therefore have a place in society and must be worthy of it. Shelley is arguing with his eye on Peacock; he has coupled Peacock's word Passion with his own word Pleasure. But again he is outrunning his brief. Another step, and he is proving that the needs which poetry answers are social needs above all, are only social needs; that man has no passions and pleasures but those which he draws from society.

The social sympathies, or those laws from which as from its elements society results, begin to develop themselves from the moment that two human beings coexist; the future is contained within the present as the plant within the seed; and equality, diversity, unity, contrast, mutual dependence, become the principles alone capable of affording the motives according to which the will of a social being is determined to action, inasmuch as he is social; and constitute pleasure in sensation, virtue in sentiment, beauty in art, truth in reasoning, and love in the intercourse of kind.

This passage is not easy to follow, because Shelley flinches from his own meaning in it. His meaning is that man in society comes to be moved only by social feelings. These social feelings, which had begun merely as 'an additional class of emotions', in the end master man's feelings and pleasure, and

become the principles alone capable of affording the motives according to which the will of a social being is determined to action.

Shelley flinches from the word 'alone' long enough to hedge this sentence with the words 'inasmuch as he is social'. It may be that Shelley, who was careless with such words, wrote this to mean 'in so far as he is social'. Even if he did so, his hedging has no force. For he tells us himself that in so far as man is not social, he is no more than an animal. In so far as he is not social, he can act only by sensation, sentiment, the intercourse of kind. The social feelings alone change these animal acts to the manly acts of pleasure, virtue, love. Nor can man for long be other than social, even in part. The social feelings lie within any two men 'as the plant within the seed', and they grow as surely as the plant grows. Man must be social, and all that is worthy in him must take its shape from his social being.

This is the base of Shelley's theory of the imagination. It is from here that Shelley takes the farther steps of his theory. Hitherto, he has said only that there is an imagination. There is a scale by which the child chooses to chuckle rather than to howl, or the poet chooses his words.

Every inflexion of tone and gesture will bear exact relation to a corresponding antitype in the pleasurable impressions which awakened it; it will be the reflected image of that impression.

Now Shelley sets out to find this scale. To do so, he looks for that which makes pleasure greatest; and finds that the greatness of pleasure lies in its order. Like Peacock's reason, Shelley's imagination is to be a principle of ordering. As it acts to make pleasure lasting, so it is to act to make it greatest. What is the principle of ordering by which this is to be done?

To find this principle, we must read together some scattered sentences in the *Defence of Poetry*. They are sentences in which Shelley is following Sidney's *Defence of Poesie*; and they are the more enlightening, because they show the changes which Shelley makes in Sidney's argument. I recall that Sidney had claimed that poets have been thought more than manly, and to have something prophetic or godly in their writing. Shelley also claims that a poet 'essentially has the character' of a prophet:

> For he not only beholds intensely the present as it is, and discovers those laws according to which present things ought to be ordered, but he beholds the future in the present, and his thoughts are the germs of the flower and the fruit of latest time.

We have met the image of the seed and the fruit before, and we shall meet it again. Here it is the image of the poet's thought. Sidney had found this thought prophetic or godly, because it holds an ideal like the ideal of God. Shelley also finds it prophetic:

because it foretells the future. Shelley does honestly believe that he is saying what Sidney said. He believes it the more firmly because his reading of Sidney is of a piece. Sidney said that poetry is better than history, because it is less particular. Shelley echoes the claim.

The one is partial, and applies only to a definite period of time, and a certain combination of events which can never again recur; the other is universal, and contains within itself the germ of a relation to whatever motives or actions have place in the possible varieties of human nature.

Again we have the image of the seed, and again we are told that the poet knows laws to shape the present and the future. And now we learn what these laws are. They are the laws which rule 'whatever motives or actions have place in the possible varieties of human nature'. What poetry offers is a formula, wider in time and place than others, for the motives or actions of men. Thus does it find the shape of present and future. This is the field which it holds among Peacock's sciences. Shelley is staking one of poetry's earliest claims in the new field of psychology.

Shelley follows this claim with an answer to the charge that poetry is immoral. Peacock had not made this charge. In the two hundred and fifty years between Gosson and Peacock, there had been written those grave poems the lack of which Gosson had cried down. Peacock therefore did not think of raising Gosson's charge that poems are 'amarous', and make the reader wanton. He would have smiled at the charge. But Shelley is writing too close to Sidney's

Defence of Poesie to look up. And the echo is enlightening. It leads Shelley to claim that poetry,
far from being immoral, is the source and keeper of
morals. Shelley, we see, is recalling another of Sidney's
claims: that poetry is the source of Virtue. This
claim has a meaning if we understand by Virtue that
ideal which Sidney set out. As Shelley reads it, however, virtue is no more than moral good: the formula
for good conduct. Poetry, he says, has been thought
to go counter to this formula, because men have not
understood how the formula is learnt. They have
thought that it is learnt by example and theory, and
they have not found these in poems. But moral good
is learnt otherwise.

The great secret of morals is love.

A man, to be greatly good, must imagine intensely and
comprehensively; he must put himself in the place of
another and of many others; the pains and pleasures of
his species must become his own. The great instrument
of moral good is the imagination; and poetry administers
to the effect by acting upon the cause.

In these sentences I read the core of Shelley's
theory of the imagination, and of the *Defence of Poetry*.
Shelley has told us that imagination is prompted by
man's need to make his pleasure lasting. He has told
us that it acts to make his pleasure greatest, by giving
order to the pleasure and to that act which the
pleasure prompts. And he has told us that, as man
becomes social, only his social feelings are worthy
to give him these pleasures. Now we learn the principle of the order which imagination gives. To imagine

intensely and comprehensively, we learn, is to 'put himself in the place of another and of many others': it is to make 'the pains and pleasures of his species his own'. The imagination is the tool of social kinship or love. It acts to make man socially good; and it does so by reminding him how others feel. Sidney had made Virtue the ideal by which man masters desire. But to Shelley, moral good is desire as it feels the desires of others. To imagine is to know the feelings and desires of others; to be good is not to outrage them. Thus, to imagine is to understand fully what is meant by being one of a society. It is to reason closely and to the end on one's place in an equal society, from the axiom 'Love thy neighbour as thyself'. No doubt the reasoning is uncommon; but Plato and Rousseau had shown that it can be carried through. Like their societies, Shelley's is a reasoned society. Shelley has said that its men must imagine. Now we learn what he means. Men must know that others feel as they do; men must reason their conduct from this knowledge. It had been Shelley's aim to prove that the imagination is as needful and worthy an act of the mind as the reason. At the end of his theory of the imagination, he has so far granted Peacock's case as to put the imagination itself within reach of the reason.

3

For Shelley, poetry is 'the expression of the imagination'; and the imagination is the act of feeling at one with one's neighbour. 'Love thy neighbour as thyself' is the act of imagination. And love is a key word to Shelley's thought. In his poems the word is rarely out of his mouth for a dozen lines. It is worth while to study the word there; and I take for study a poem on the theme of love, *Prometheus Unbound.*

Prometheus Unbound tells a simple story. Prometheus, who wants to make men happy and self-fulfilled, has taught them the use of fire, of drugs, of mechanics. For this Jupiter has punished him cruelly; for Jupiter fears men, whose power of goodness may challenge and overthrow his power. And power like Jupiter's is evil and pitiful, because it must act under the press of such fear. Prometheus, the symbol of imagination and love, feels the pity always. Always his cry is

> I weigh not what ye do, but what ye suffer,
> Being evil.

This is Prometheus's gift: to make the pains and pleasures of his species his own. He did not always use this gift. When first Jupiter chained him, he cursed Jupiter. He has forgotten the curse; and so changed is the world already, in the shadow of his pity, that he can find no one to recall it. It is symbolic that only Jupiter's own shadow double, the shadow of evil, will speak Prometheus's curse over to him. Prometheus listens, and asks the earth,

Prometheus. Were these my words, O Parent?
The Earth.   They were thine.
Prometheus. It doth repent me: words are quick and vain;
  Grief for awhile is blind, and so was mine.
  I wish no living thing to suffer pain.

This forgiveness, although it comes early in the first act, is the centre of the play. Jupiter's downfall, Prometheus's freedom, really come at this moment when Prometheus pities him and all living things. There is a striking likeness to the moment in Coleridge's *Rime of the Ancient Mariner* when the spell-bound sailor blesses the water-snakes, and so breaks free.

> O happy living things! no tongue
> Their beauty might declare:
> A spring of love gushed from my heart,
> And I blessed them unaware:
> Sure my kind saint took pity on me,
> And I blessed them unaware.
>
> The selfsame moment I could pray;
> And from my neck so free
> The Albatross fell off, and sank
> Like lead into the sea.

For Coleridge also links the imagination to love, and there finds grace, the spring of freedom.

There is little more story. Jupiter is overthrown; and the rest of the play is a mild orgy of love talk, which describes the happiness which Prometheus's love has won for man and for nature also. Except once, between Prometheus and Asia, this love is not love between man and woman. It is social love, the love of neighbours, 'the social sympathies'; that love which is 'the great secret of morals' which Shelley has underlined in the *Defence of Poetry*. We see the model of this love in Prometheus's forgiveness; and its power in the overthrow of Jupiter. A measure of Jupiter's evil is that in his reign love always draws ruin after it, because it has been cut off from the other virtues.

The wise want love; and those who love want wisdom;
And all best things are thus confused to ill.

A measure of Prometheus's goodness is that he makes all virtues one, and that one is love itself.

> There was mingled many a cry—
> Freedom! Hope! Death! Victory!
> Till they faded through the sky;
> And one sound, above, around,
> One sound beneath, around, above,
> Was moving; 'twas the soul of Love.

Love is the source of man's power and fulfilment. It is first his power over himself. By love man may shape himself and be free, as the chained Prometheus has been free in his will.

> Men walked
> One with the other even as spirits do,
> None fawned, none trampled; hate, disdain, or fear,
> Self-love, or self-contempt, on human brows
> No more inscribed.

And love is a second power: power over the world. Shelley claims that it can rule every kind of worldly happening; it can 'make the earth one brotherhood'. Love can change the nature of animals: 'it makes the reptile equal to the God'. It can bind the virtues of vegetables into a single ecstasy.

> The wild odour of the forest flowers,
> The music of the living grass and air,
> The emerald light of leaf-entangled beams

> Round its intense yet self-conflicting speed,
> Seem kneaded into one aëreal mass
> Which drowns the sense.

It can change the Earth; and it can change the Moon.
The best and oddest lyric of the play is the Moon's
love cry to the Earth,

> The snow upon my lifeless mountains
> Is loosened into living fountains,
> My solid oceans flow, and sing, and shine:
> A spirit from my heart bursts forth,
> It clothes with unexpected birth
> My cold bare bosom: Oh! it must be thine
>   On mine, on mine!
>
> Gazing on thee I feel, I know
> Green stalks burst forth, and bright flowers grow,
> And living shapes upon my bosom move:
> Music is in the sea and air,
> Wingèd clouds soar here and there,
> Dark with the rain new buds are dreaming of:
>   'Tis love, all love!

After such flights, we are not taken aback to find the
Chorus of Spirits setting off to 'colonize' the stars
on behalf of the brotherhood of love.

Love has power over man, and over nature. It has
a third power: over the gods. Shelley tells us that
Prometheus himself gave Jupiter the power which he
abused. He is saying that man makes his own gods,
by his imagination. Man is enough for himself in
all fields, and above all in his thought. There are no
men in *Prometheus Unbound*, only undying shapes,
furies, fairies, phantoms, spirits; yet all are thought
of as the servants of the will of man. All are

> Those subtle and fair spirits,
> Whose homes are the dim caves of human thought,
> And who inhabit, as birds wing the wind,
> Its world-surrounding aether.

No one of them is such an ideal as man must strive to win and to be worthy of. All are the kindly thoughts which men may have so soon as they are free of the mechanical hardships of Jupiter's reign,

> Famine, and then toil, and then disease.

I have traced this theory through the *Defence of Poetry* as Shelley's theory of the imagination. I find it again in *Prometheus Unbound* as the theory of love: love is the core of Shelley's imagination. The imagination is the act by which man seeks to make his pleasures lasting and to make them greatest, by giving order to them. There are no models for this order, and no ideals. There is only man's own principle of order,

he must put himself in the place of another and of many others; the pains and pleasures of his species must become his own.

It is the principle of neighbourly love; it is a social principle. When Shelley looks forward, in the *Defence of Poetry*, in *Prometheus Unbound*, or elsewhere, he looks forward to a better society. It is not merely that he believes that no good can grow without a bettering of society; all honest men must believe that. Shelley believes that every good will grow of itself from the bettering of society; that there is no good but the bettering of society. Jupiter has no evil but that he sets himself against this bettering; because Shelley knows no evil but to be anti-social, and no good but to be social. That is why the key word of evil in Shelley is always tyranny, and the key word of good is love.

Such a theory cannot defend poetry. In this theory, only that is good which has a social use. It was on this theory that Peacock charged poetry: because it has no social use. Peacock said that society is to be made by reasoning. This may be less true of the society of Peacock's day than he hoped. It is the more true of the ideal society towards which Shelley looked: the society of Plato or of Rousseau. And Plato had said that poetry has no place in such a society. Shelley may call the kind of reasoning which is needed love, or he may call it imagination. But in the end he can claim for it only this, that it is the reasoning of one who

must put himself in the place of another and of many others; the pains and pleasures of his species must become his own.

No doubt reasoners rarely do this; but it remains the business of reasoners.

Shelley himself knew this. He knew that his faith was in reason and in science. He knew that he was serious when he saw the imagination as a power to colonize the stars. He knew that his greatest claim for Prometheus, symbol of love and imagination, was that he with

Science struck the thrones of earth and heaven;

that
> He told the hidden power of herbs and springs,
> And Disease drank and slept. Death grew like sleep.
> He taught the implicated orbits woven
> Of the wide-wandering stars.
>
> He taught to rule, as life directs the limbs,
> The tempest-wingèd chariots of the Ocean,
> And the Celt knew the Indian. Cities then
> Were built.
>
> Such, the alleviations of his state,
> Prometheus gave to man.

Then why should he have claimed these powers for the poet, of all men?

It is a question which Shelley would not think out. He liked poetry; but his faith was in science. Therefore he must believe that poetry was somehow a help to science, and a kind of science. He must claim that the poet somehow has a flair for doing the job of scientists. And these are his serious and his highest claims for him: that like Prometheus, he is doctor, astronomer, pilot, builder. He is 'the unacknowledged legislator of the world'; and more,

> For he not only beholds intensely the present as it is, and discovers those laws according to which present things ought to be ordered, but he beholds the future in the present, and his thoughts are the germs of the flower and the fruit of latest time.

I have remarked how often Shelley uses this image of the seed and the fruit. Strikingly it throws up his troubled, double feeling. On the one hand, it is the image of an act of nature, working within laws of science which will at last be mapped as surely as the course of a star. On the other hand, it is the image of a living act, whose laws are only partly known, and whose mapping is still something of guesswork and adventure. Such a borderland, Shelley feels, is the land of the poet. Here science is at its beginning; and here the flair of the experimenter is its most worthy and spectacular help. Shelley's imagination is this flair.

This belief cannot stand against Peacock's case. Peacock claimed that the time spent in reading and writing poems would be better spent in the work of science. If the poetic imagination is merely a flair in the outfields of science, in botany or psychology, Peacock's claim is just. For then the laws on which the poet is at work: 'those laws according to which present things ought to be ordered' and by which we can 'behold the future in the present'; the laws of 'whatever motives or actions have place in the possible varieties of human nature'; the laws by which the poet 'puts himself in the place of another and of many others' and makes 'the pains and pleasures of his species his own'; all these laws are laws of science. They can be found by the methods of science; and the haphazard work of the poet is out of place in them. Once we grant Peacock that every field of thought and of living can at last be mapped by science, we have no answer to his claim that poetry day by day grows out of date and useless. For then they are the fields of reasoners and of scientists; and poets have business there only so long as the reasoners are learning their jobs. Poets have business there only because they have a flair for these jobs, as calculating prodigies have a flair for doing sums. But the way to do sums remains the way of reasoning, and the calculating prodigies are not on the path of mathematical progress. If Shelley may claim that this flair makes poets useful to-day, he must the more surely grant that they will be useless to-morrow. He must grant just Peacock's claim, that

as the sciences of morals and of mind advance towards perfection, as they become more enlarged and comprehensive in their views, as reason gains the ascendancy in them over imagination and feeling, poetry can no longer accompany them in their progress, but drops into the back ground, and leaves them to advance alone.

Shelley tries hard to run away from this claim. He tries at all costs to find poetry useful. Towards the end of the *Defence of Poetry*, he even sets up a new meaning of the word Use, which shall be larger than Peacock's meaning and by which poetry may be useful. Now there can be no doubt what meaning of use Peacock and Shelley have in mind. In this meaning, to be useful must be to further the growth and the being of the society towards which the writer looks. But Shelley, looking to that Platonic society of reason from which poets were so surely banished, tries to dodge this meaning. He reaches back to the pleasure on which he has built his theory of the imagination, and he claims,

The production and assurance of pleasure in this highest sense is true utility.

Since nothing is said about this highest sense of pleasure except that 'it is difficult to define', and is often found in pain, the claim is not serious. Shelley himself is scamping it. Coleridge made a like claim, and was better able to uphold it; and I shall speak of the claim when I study his theory of imagination. Shelley has run away from the argument; and the last pages of the *Defence of Poetry* are the sad litter of his flight. They pile climax upon climax. They make boasts without backing and without meaning. They are studded with sentences which no album can be without:

Poetry is indeed something divine. It is at once the centre and circumference of knowledge.

Poetry is the record of the best and happiest moments of the happiest and best minds.

It arrests the vanishing apparitions which haunt the interlunations of life, and veiling them, or in language or in form, sends them forth among mankind, bearing sweet news of kindred joy to those with whom their sisters abide.

Poets are the unacknowledged legislators of the world. These sentences show that Shelley liked poetry, and that he thought others would be better for liking it. They show nothing else. To Shelley, the good of man was to be found in a good society: and a good society was a society shaped by reason,

> When Reason's voice,
> Loud as the voice of Nature, shall have waked
> The nations; and mankind perceive that vice
> Is discord, war, and misery; that virtue
> Is peace, and happiness and harmony.

Long before Peacock, Plato had said that poetry serves no good in such a society. Nothing that Shelley says answers Peacock and Plato.

JOHN DRYDEN

JOHN DRYDEN

I

BETWEEN the time of Sidney and the time of Dryden, English poetry grew masterful twice: in the Elizabethan playwrights, and in Milton. Dryden first knew the worth of these masters, who were to be the masters of English poetry. And Dryden held to the worth which he knew. There are readers who find Dryden's poems dull for lacking the accent of these masters. These readers mistake him. Dryden had masters, not models. And his masters taught him no brogue because they did not teach him to speak but to think. Dryden knew that his speech was sharper than theirs.

The master who taught Dryden most was Ben Jonson. Jonson had taught others: Elizabethan playwrights and Cavalier poets. They had stood in the shadow of Jonson because they had found his judgment helpful. But Dryden stands closer to Jonson than this: he stands in Jonson's mind. The great names which bounded Jonson's mind bound Dryden's mind. The principles which ruled Jonson's mind rule Dryden's mind. To study Dryden is first to study Jonson.

Ben Jonson was proud of being a scholar. But he was not a scholar from pride, or by trade. He was a scholar because he took pleasure in good writers and good thinkers. His was the growing, everyday

pleasure which the Elizabethans came to take in the
ancients. They came to understand, to take for their
own, and to change for their own ends, the thought
of the ancients. They changed their own thought and
their own speech; they made common the speech of
the ancients. The change is larger in Elizabethan
speech than in thought: for no age could have made
the ancients so common which did not seem to itself
already to be at one with them in thought. Thus we
shall seldom find Sidney and Jonson thinking differently; but we shall find them speaking differently.

Like Sidney, Jonson holds an ideal of poetry. He
does not hold it in Sidney's word Virtue. Jonson
writes,

> *Knowledge* is the action of the *Soule*; and is perfect
> without the *senses*, as having the seeds of all *Science*, and
> *Vertue* in its selfe: but not without the service of the *senses*:
> by those Organs, the *Soule workes*: She is a perpetuall
> Agent, prompt and subtile.

This is Sidney's belief, that there is an ideal which
can rule the mind, although it must work through
the senses. But the ideal is not named Virtue: the
word Virtue, like the word Science, stands only for
a worldly conduct here. Jonson has put his ideal into
the word Knowledge; and Jonson has said of that
which is known,

> *Truth* is mans proper good; and the onely *immortall*
> thing, was given to our mortality to use.

Jonson sees the seat of this ideal in the soul, and
the seat of the worldly in the senses. Like Sidney's,

Jonson's thought is founded in the two-ness of the soul and the senses. Only because there is this two-ness does poetry have a worth which is unlike the worth of other arts.

Poetry, and *Picture*, are Arts of a like nature; and both are busie about imitation.

For they both invent, faine, and devise many things, and accomodate all they invent to the use, and service of nature. Yet of the two, the Pen is more noble, then the Pencill. For that can speake to the Understanding; the other, but to the Sense.

Understanding here has the meaning which Jonson has given to Knowledge: it is the ideal 'action of the *Soule*'. And Jonson holds fast to Sidney's belief that poetry is a source of this ideal, and is the business of the soul. Only in one way does Jonson's claim differ from Sidney's. Jonson does allow the senses to have their own being, and he does not think that this being is worthless. The senses may be pleased without touching the soul: as in painting. Sidney did not think such pleasure worth speaking of. But to Jonson it does have some right, and makes its own art. We may see in this the first step along that road at the end of which Shelley held that poetry and the soul itself are made up only of such pleasures.

The word Knowledge or Understanding carries a hint that Jonson drew his theory of an ideal from Plato. And the sentence,

Knowledge is the action of the *Soule*; and is perfect without the *senses*, as having the seeds of all *Science*, and *Vertue* in its selfe,

may be taken to sum Plato's theory of knowledge,
which holds that the soul at birth has known all
that the senses slowly and only partly uncover in life.
But it was Aristotle rather than Plato who taught
Jonson. Jonson's *Discoveries* ends with a painstaking
summary of Aristotle's *Poetics*; and principles from
the *Poetics* are everywhere in Jonson's writing. The
likening of poetry and painting which I have quoted
has recalled such a principle: the principle of Imitation. We have met this principle in Sidney, and we
have seen that Sidney was ill at ease with it. Jonson
was better able than Sidney to fit it into the Elizabethan scheme. It was Jonson who made Imitation
part of English criticism. From Jonson, rather than
from the French and Latin critics, Dryden learned
it; and thence it went to measure the orderly building
of Augustan writing.

Sidney had not thought deeply about Imitation:
'that is to say, a representing, counterfeiting, or
figuring forth', he called it. It was clear to him that
poetry must counterfeit; and there was no more to
be said than this. When Sidney did say more, and
tried to make Imitation 'to delight & teach', he
found himself tangled in contradictions. Jonson is
not content with this. He must go deeper; he must
unravel the contradictions. Like Sidney, Jonson believes that poetry makes 'an other nature': this makes
poetry more worthy than painting, which speaks only
from the nature known to the senses. Painting imitates
the known nature; then what does poetry imitate?
Clearly, answers Jonson, it imitates the other nature.

But the other nature is thought out by the poet himself. If this is Imitation, then to imitate is merely to think aloud: it is to put into words a nature which may change from day to day and from poet to poet. The speaking of thoughts cannot be called Imitation; unless they are thoughts which also lie outside the mind of the poet. Only so can we couple Imitation with the belief in 'an other nature': if we believe that the other nature which the poet thinks out and imitates has an absolute being, beyond his thought.

Jonson does believe this. He does believe that the other nature is an ideal outside the poet. It is such an ideal as Plato's Knowledge, towards which Jonson has looked: which is in being outside man, and which man makes only in that he grows aware of it. Jonson believes that when the poet thinks, he merely grows aware of that other nature of which he thinks; and therefore he does not so much make his other nature, as imitate it. This is Jonson's theory of Imitation; the theory which Dryden made common, and which the Augustans overthrew.

We see that Sidney and Jonson are not altogether at one in this. They are at one in their root thought, that poetry is an ideal which is outside the world of the senses. But they do not look on this ideal in the same way. To Sidney, the poet makes 'an other nature'; Sidney's stress is on the poet's gift of making. To Jonson, the poet sees Nature, and it is 'an other nature' not seen by the eye; Jonson's stress is on the poet's gift of seeing. Sidney looks on the ideal actively as made by the poet; his name for it is therefore the active word Virtue. Jonson looks on the ideal passively as seen by the poet; his name for it is therefore the passive word Nature. To him, the poet is

the interpreter, and arbiter of nature, a teacher of things diuine, no lesse then humane.

We must be sure of Jonson's meaning here. In three hundred years, the word Nature has had a dozen meanings. In our minds it fits into such couplings as 'the natural man' and 'nature study', in which its aptness is to the world of the senses. This has been so since the Augustans: and from this cause they misunderstood and overthrew Jonson's and Dryden's theory of Imitation. But it was not so for Jonson. For Jonson, Nature was that which the poet imitated; and since it was plain to Jonson that the poet did not imitate the world of the senses, it followed that Nature was the field of the soul. This was that other nature of which Sidney had spoken; and although Jonson did not see it like Sidney, this was his Nature also.

I underline this meaning because we find it hard to hold in mind. We find it hard to understand that Nature has not always meant the great world of the senses; that Jonson could have been so odd as to mean by it the field of the soul. Yet only if we understand this shall we understand Jonson's round claims,

I cannot thinke *Nature* is so spent, and decay'd, that she can bring forth nothing worth her former yeares. She is always the same, like her selfe: And when she collects her strength, is abler still. Men are decay'd, and *studies*: Shee is not.

This is pointless if *Nature* is the nature of Gray or of Wordsworth. For then it claims merely that this nature can still make swedes and eclipses at least as big as those of former years: and this claim has nothing to do with 'Men, and *studies*'. If the claim is to mean anything, we must read it otherwise. We must read it as a claim that the other nature of the poet is such a Nature as I have been reading in Jonson, an absolute nature from which all men may draw at all times. They no longer draw as they did because they have weakened. Not poetry has grown worse, but poets; not Nature, but men, through whom she must work. And this is plain if we set by its side the sentence which I have quoted:

Knowledge is the action of the *Soule*; and is perfect without the *senses*,
but not without the service of the *senses*: by those Organs, the *Soule workes*.

For this sentence sets out within the small world of man himself the same play of ideal and actual which Jonson finds in the large world. The ideal is unchanged, and holds hidden within itself all that the actual can ever uncover. But the ideal cannot work, it cannot be uncovered, except by the actual. The ideal shapes and drives the actual; yet it is at the mercy of the actual. In the small world of man, the ideal is the soul and the actual is the senses. In the large world, the ideal is Nature and the actual is man.

I find this thought in Dryden as in Jonson: this is the thought in which Dryden grew up. Dryden

speaks less of it, because this is not what he built but
what he built upon. He quotes as a matter of course
from Bellori,

Nature always intends a consummate beauty in her
productions, yet through the inequality of the matter
the forms are altered.

For which reason, the artful painter and the sculptor,
imitating the Divine Maker, form to themselves, as well
as they are able, a model of the superior beauties.

This idea, which we may call the goddess of painting
and of sculpture, descends upon the marble and the cloth,
and becomes the original of those arts; and being measured
by the compass of the intellect, is itself the measure of
the performing hand; and being animated by the imagination, infuses life into the image. The idea of the painter
and sculptor is undoubtedly that perfect and excellent
example of the mind, by imitation of which imagined
form all things are represented which fall under human
sight.

Dryden is quoting his own thought:

Nature; a thing so almost Infinite, and Boundless, as
can never fully be Comprehended, but where the Images
of all things are always present.

It must be an idea of perfection, from which both the
epic poet and the history painter draws.

It is the thought of his simplest sentences,

> To be like Nature, is to be set above it,

of the 'high imitation of Nature in those sudden gusts
of passion'; the thought of that 'Nature wrought up
to an higher pitch' of which every essay speaks. It
is the thought of Nature which Dryden took from
Jonson.

Nevertheless Dryden's thought is not all of a piece with Jonson's; it is not of a piece with itself. There is one line along which it has begun to crack. For Sidney, there had been moments when the ideal could shape the social good: and in these high moments man learned Virtue. Perhaps for Jonson already these moments were too rare, and the crack between the ideal and the social good of Elizabethan times too plain. Virtue was becoming a word of no world, and Jonson seldom uses it. For Dryden certainly, this cracking silenced the word Virtue. It was becoming harder to think that man could make or could even see the ideal at all. It was becoming too hard to link Nature to the nature of man; and soon the Augustans gave it up, and spoke only of the nature of man. Dryden still held together, as if by force, the breaking world. He still held to an ideal Nature, and he still held that the poet could see and imitate this ideal. But to do so, he had to understand his ideal Nature by way of the nature of man. He had to balance two meanings which no one again was strong enough, and subtle enough, to hold together. I have set out the one meaning, which Dryden took from Jonson. I turn to the other meaning, which Dryden made.

2

Dryden uses the word Nature more loosely than Jonson. These loose uses trap him into those endless debates, in which he urges on one side 'that Rhyme is best or most natural for a serious subject'; and

then asks on the other, 'whether Rhyme be nearest
the nature of what it represents'. And there are
other uses which we are tempted to bundle with these.
Jonson has written,

I cannot thinke *Nature* is so spent, and decay'd, that
she can bring forth nothing worth her former yeares.
She is always the same, like her selfe.

When Dryden makes this claim, he writes,

Mankind is ever the same, and nothing lost out of
Nature, though every thing is alter'd.

Surely Dryden does not mean the Nature which
Jonson has meant. If Dryden is not writing very
loosely, he means the nature of man; and Jonson
has set his Nature flatly against this:

Men are decay'd, and *studies*: Shee is not.

True, Jonson and Dryden are writing about different
things. Jonson is writing about poetry. Dryden is
praising the freshness of the pictures of men and
women in Chaucer. But the puzzle is still there.
Why should Dryden think that these men and women
make up Nature? Why should he choose to praise
Chaucer because he drew lifelike men and women?

These are searching questions. We have grown
used to hearing books praised because the men and
women in them are lifelike. Three hundred years of
criticism of Shakespeare, for example, have taught us
to speak of him as a maker of characters. But Dryden
was among the first to speak of him thus. Dryden was
a pioneer of the search for character. Why? And
how can character be coupled with his ideal Nature?

We begin to answer these questions when we recall that Dryden was a playwright. Dryden was the last English poet who was a playwright by trade; and the last English playwright who was a poet first. Before Dryden, the playwrights had been poets, and for long the only poets. Willy nilly, the play to them was poetry; and their plays are to be judged by the standards of poetry. After Dryden, the playwrights were not poets. Their minds were given to the play only. Dryden hung between the two standards. All his life he carried on such debates as those of the *Essay of Dramatick Poesie*. All his life he swung from one side to the other in the debates, because he was trying to judge by two standards at once. He wanted to judge the play and the poem together; and therefore he could not keep his judgment of the play free of the standards of poetry, nor his judgment of poetry free of the standards of the play. And once or twice he did prove that the two can be made one: that the poetry need not master the play as it had done for the Elizabethans, and that the play need not master all else as it has done for us. *All for Love* is such a proof; and we may set it by the side of Shakespeare's *Antony and Cleopatra*, and of George Bernard Shaw's *Caesar and Cleopatra*, to see how rare a balance it strikes.

Dryden's judgment of poetry is therefore shaped by the needs of the play. The play more than another kind of writing is the forcing ground of character. Here Dryden learned to look for lifelike men and women, because here he needed them as the tools

for his writing. Here he learned to think of his ideal
Nature as resting upon the nature of man. Dryden
does claim that human nature is the centre of every
kind of poem: 'the Soul of Poesie, which is imitation
of humour and passions', he writes in the *Essay of
Dramatick Poesie*. It is enlightening that he should
make the claim there. For it shows us again that the
claim grows from the claim that the play is 'the
Soul of Poesie'; the claim is rooted in the play.
I quote from the same essay,

A Play ought to be, *A just and lively Image of Humane
Nature, representing its Passions and Humours.*

Dryden is unhappy between Nature and human
nature. He wants to make an ideal Nature which
shall have its seat in the nature of man. And the
wish has sprung in him from the wish to couple poetry
and play.

I have said that in *All for Love* Dryden seems to
me to have fulfilled this wish, in fact. I think that
he also fulfilled it in his theory. I think that he did
for some moments raise the nature of man to an
ideal Nature; and that we only understand his standards, his Wit and Judgment, if we understand that
they are held together by these moments. We only
understand the break-down of these standards in the
Augustans if we understand that there was then no
such theory to hold them together.

In the *Essay of Dramatick Poesie* Dryden praises
Shakespeare because he held to Nature. This praise
has a long history, from Heminge and Condell to

to-day. Ben Jonson, Milton, Pope, Thomson, Samuel Johnson, Coleridge: each praised Shakespeare because he followed Nature, and each meant something different by his Nature. To Dryden, this Nature is in part human nature; he writes that Shakespeare 'look'd inwards, and found her there'. Nevertheless, it is a Nature which wears Jonson's cloth. For what Shakespeare found when he looked inwards was 'the largest and most comprehensive soul'; and Dryden leaves no doubt that, like Jonson, he is speaking of a poetic soul: he writes that Shakespeare had

undoubtedly a larger Soul of Poesie, than ever any of our Nation.

What is uncommon, then, is not merely the ideal meaning which Dryden has given to Nature: but the meaning which he now gives to the inward, human nature. Dryden sees human nature not as the sum of acts and conduct, nor as those 'pains and pleasures of his species' which Shelley saw. He sees a greater link between men. To find this link, we must read what Dryden writes about plays.

Dryden writes,

Every alteration or crossing of a design, every new sprung passion, and turn of it, is a part of the action, and much the noblest, except we conceive nothing to be action till they come to blows; as if the painting of the Heroes mind were not more properly the Poets work then the strength of his body.

This tells us that a writer must rule the characters of his play by high ends. It does more. It hints

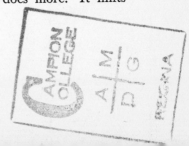

at the kind of ends, and at the kind of link between men which is Dryden's human nature. It does so in the claim that the painting of the hero's mind is the poet's work. For the painting of which Dryden is speaking is Imitation; he is bracketing into one word the likening of *Poetry*, and *Picture*, which had been made since Imitation was first spoken of. And what is imitated here is a cast of mind, common to the minds of men yet re-made in each. When Dryden makes the same claim again in the *Essay of Dramatick Poesie*, that the play has higher ends than the acts of its characters,

The Audience; who watch the movements of their minds, as much as the changes of their fortunes,

he again adds as a matter of course,

For the imaging of the first is properly the work of a Poet.

Imaging also stands for Imitation. Like Jonson, Dryden thinks of the Imitation by the poet not as a making, but as a seeing; the word Imaging is more passive than Imitation. But what is imaged? Another nature, said Jonson: a Nature which is in being outside the poet. Dryden also said this; but he was harder put to it to say what being such a Nature could have. With his playwright's eyes he saw that the better poets, among the Elizabethans for example, were the very poets who saw better the minds of their characters. And so he came to answer that the other nature which poets see, better or worse, is the root

nature of the mind. They do not see the mind of this
man or that, nor even the mind of this kind of man
or that kind; but they see that root mind which all
minds have in common, and from which all mind
springs. They see not the natures of men, but the
Nature of mind which moves man himself. And this,
in Dryden, is the Nature which poets imitate.

Dryden understood that to give to the ideal of
Nature this simple meaning carries danger. A Nature
which stands for the common and root mind of man
will in the end surely be debased to the everyday,
human nature. The poet who holds before him an
ideal pattern of mind will give way, step by step,
to the poet who pieces together the minds of others,
who 'puts himself in the place of another and of
many others' and who thus makes 'the pains and
pleasures of his species his own'. Dryden is on the
road which leads to Shelley, and on which Nature
becomes the nature of men. We can judge the nature
of men only by their acts, which alone allow us to
look into and to image their minds. We are therefore
in danger of using poetry to image only conduct.
We have come back to the threat which Sidney
fought, that poetry may become merely a tool in
the making of social conduct. Dryden also fought
this threat, always by pitting the root mind of man
against the mere conduct of men:

Every alteration or crossing of a design, every new
sprung passion, and turn of it, is a part of the action,
and much the noblest, except we conceive nothing to
be action till they come to blows.

Under this sentence runs a fierce belief that there is a content of the mind and passions greater than that which spills into the acts of men. And when Dryden ends the like claim,

> The Audience; who watch the movements of their minds, as much as the changes of their fortunes. For the imaging of the first is properly the work of a Poet,

with the words,

> the latter he borrows of the Historian,

he is using for his belief Aristotle's own belief, which Sidney had used: the belief that poetry

> is more Philosophicall and more [studiously serious] then History.

Dryden finds this Philosophy in those 'movements of their minds' in which, to him, men show their root mind. And they are movements beyond their acts, and only the poet images them. It is to the point to recall the ground on which Dryden upheld Aristotle and the Ancients.

> Those Springs of humane Nature are not so easily discover'd by every superficial Judge: It requires Philosophy as well as Poetry, to sound the depth of all the Passions; what they are in themselves, and how they are to be provok'd: and in this Science the best Poets have excell'd.

This belief of Dryden's also springs from Jonson: it springs from Jonson's theory of humours. We sometimes think of Jonson's humours as single strands of the mind, enlarged to make a one-sided character, of the kind which we might meet in the case-book of a psychologist. Coleridge calls them 'the hopeless patients of a mad-doctor'. And Dryden himself, in the *Essay of Dramatick Poesie*, thinks of them thus. He is mistaken. Jonson's humours are single strands of the mind; but they are not the strands which psychology unravels from the mind. Rather they are the strands which ethics finds in the mind: the virtues and vices which Spenser set out in the *Faerie Queene*. The great humours of Volpone, and Mosca, and Morose, have no singleness or truth in psychology. They have the air of truth, because they are lively and delightful: because, within the play, they are alive. But they are not socially alive; they do not make the common world; they have no meaning in a science which studies only conduct. They are Vices, in the meaning of the Morality plays. And this is the meaning of those 'manners' in which Dryden finds his *Grounds of Criticism in Tragedy*. The strands which Dryden finds in the mind are not the psychological, social strands. They are Jonson's humours. They are the strands of ideal virtues and vices, and by them the mind fixes its own worth. The mind so fixed, this root mind of man, is Dryden's Nature. This is the faith which Dryden sets out when he writes,

Moral Truth is the Mistress of the Poet, as much as of the Philosopher. Poesie must resemble Natural truth, but it must *be* Ethical.

Dryden is using the word 'natural' loosely here. But his belief is clear: that the truth of poetry, that truth which elsewhere he calls Nature, is a truth in the mind which is absolute, and whose model is ethical virtue.

For Dryden, Nature is an ideal mind. It is an orderly Nature, and its order is the order of the mind. The nature given us by the senses has no order. All Dryden's writings and acts show that he stood in horror of disorder. This is the horror which runs under his changes of party and faith. This is the horror which fills his fiercest writing.

No Government has ever been, or even can be, wherein Timeservers and Blockheads will not be uppermost. The persons are only chang'd, but the same juglings in State, the same Hypocrisie in Religion, the same Self-Interest, and Mis-mannagement, will remain for ever. Blood and Mony will be lavish'd in all Ages, only for the Preferment of new Faces, with old Consciences. There is too often a Jaundise in the Eyes of Great Men; they see not those whom they raise in the same Colours with other Men. All whom they affect, look Golden to them.

It is because he fears this disorder of the world of the senses that Dryden must set his Nature in the mind. The Lucretian order of the world is not enough; only a greater mind can truly order the world. Dryden writes *To my Honored Friend Sir Robert Howard On His Excellent Poems,*

> This is a piece too fair
> To be the child of Chance, and not of Care.
> No Atoms casually together hurl'd
> Could e're produce so beautifull a world.
> Nor dare I such a doctrine here admit,
> As would destroy the providence of wit.

Dryden sees each poem as a world, in which a lesser part pleases the senses. But this world of the senses, of chance excitements, cannot be beautiful unless it has an order of the mind, in a greater mind. This alone is its worth. Only so do we see Nature in the world: only so do we make Wit in the poem.

The words Wit and Judgment are puzzling in Dryden and in the Augustans; more puzzling, because more haphazard, than the Imitation of Nature. There is a world of change between Dryden's sharp meaning,

> No Atoms casually together hurl'd
> Could e're produce so beautifull a world.
> Nor dare I such a doctrine here admit,
> As would destroy the providence of wit,

and the commonplace of Pope,

> True Wit is Nature to advantage dress'd.

To Dryden, Wit is not Nature 'dress'd': it is a principle which fills and orders nature, so that the world of the poet's senses becomes the Nature of his mind. Dryden does use the word Wit loosely, as he uses the word Nature loosely; and the looseness underlines the likeness of the two words. What Nature is outside the poet's mind, that Wit is inside; and as Nature at times sinks to mean the natural world of the senses, so Wit at times sinks to mean a sensuous excess of imagination. This last is the meaning which we know best, because it is the meaning given to Wit by the Augustans. To the Augustans, all the words Nature,

Wit, Fancy, Invention, Genius, came at last to mean only one thing: lack of tidiness and of Art. Dryden never sinks to this meaning. In Dryden's belief, the poet sees or images an ideal mind outside himself which is Nature. He makes a model of this ideal in his own mind; and this is Wit.

The Composition of all Poems is or ought to be of wit; and wit in the Poet, or wit writing (if you will give me leave to use a School distinction), is no other than the faculty of imagination in the Writer; which, like a nimble Spaniel, beats over and ranges through the field of Memory, till it springs the Quarry it hunted after; or, without metaphor, which searches over all the Memory for the Species or Ideas of those things which it designs to represent. Wit written, is that which is well defin'd, the happy result of Thought, or product of Imagination.

Dryden is not writing of the '*mechanical* memory' which Coleridge couples with the fancy. He is writing of the memory of Plato, an imaginative memory: the sleeping memory of the soul's life into which we reach back for our understanding of 'the Species or Ideas' of all things. Wit is the imagination by which the poet reaches the root mind and memory of man, Nature. Wit is thus the Nature which the poet makes or imagines, from the nature which he sees or images.

The fear which Dryden has, lest Nature might seem to be disorderly, therefore carries with it a fear lest Wit may grow disorderly. True, Wit is of the mind and not of the senses; and when he speaks of the providence of wit, Dryden means the ordering mind. But Wit is too close to the wild nature of the senses, whose touch Dryden wards off fearfully. Wit is therefore ruled by another ordering act of the poet's mind: the Judgment.

We remember the word Judgment as part of Dryden's dreary quarrels between rhyme and no rhyme: that rhyme 'gives the Judgment its busiest Employment'; that 'he who wants judgment to confine his fancy in blank Verse, may want it as much in Rhyme'. But even in these quarrels, it had a noble history. I quote from Samuel Daniel's *Defence of Ryme*.

When we heare Musicke, we must be in our eare, in the vtter-roome of sense, but when we intertaine iudgement, we retire into the cabinet and innermost withdrawing chamber of the soule: And it is but as Musicke for the eare, *Verba sequi fidibus modulanda Latinis.* but it is a worke of power for the soule. *Numerósque modósque ediscere vitæ.*

Daniel is setting the Judgment against the senses, to rule the nature given by the senses. This is the meaning which I read in Ben Jonson's claim,

To judge of Poets is only the facultie of Poets; and not of all Poets, but the best.

For if this is to be more than a boast, it must mean that the act of judging the thought of a poet is itself a poetic act, without which no poem is written. We come nearest to this meaning in speech when we say that a sudden bodily act, a spurt or a catch, has been well judged. We mean that the single act of hand or eye has been placed of itself under the whole man, and led by the whole man. This is like the meaning of Daniel and of Jonson; and Dryden follows their meaning. Dryden's Judgment is the ruling and leading, by the whole poetic soul, of the single acts and gifts which go to make the poem. Dryden does not make the large claim of Jonson; he will only say,

Poets themselves are the most proper, though I conclude not the only Critiques.

Nevertheless, he finds that others 'have too narrow Souls to judge of Poetry'. For him, as for Daniel and Jonson, Judgment brings the Platonic soul to bear on the poem. Jonson has seen the act of this soul as Knowledge; Dryden also finds it in the mind. And the mind can only see Nature and make Wit by virtue of the Judgment. For Dryden,

Judgment is indeed the Master-workman in a Play.

In Dryden's belief, the Judgment has therefore an outstanding place. It is not a pruning tool, with which the extravagances of Wit are to be lopped off: this became its use only in the narrow thought of the Augustans. It is not an act of setting right at all, which takes place after the poem has been thought out. Dryden does hold that the Judgment works best when it works without haste; he writes of the Judgment,

The Poet examines that most which he produceth with the greatest Leisure, and which, he knows, must pass the severest Test of the Audience, because they are aptest to have it ever in their Memory: as the Stomach makes the best Concoction when it strictly embraces the Nourishment, and takes account of every little Particle as it passes through.

But the likening to the stomach shows that Dryden does not think of the Judgment as a setting right by one gift of that which has been made by another. Rather the Judgment is an act which is whole, like the whole digestion; and it is an act by the whole poet, as if by the whole process of the stomach. Judgment is the act by which the poet places his sight of nature under his soul; and by which he rules and leads the making of his own Nature, which is his Wit. Judgment is the act of Imitation of the poet's own Nature or Wit. It is the act by which he holds together the passive Imitation of Nature, and the active making of Wit.

In Dryden's theory, the making of the poem has thus been shifted from the Imitation to the Wit and thence to the Judgment. Therefore the tools with which Dryden tests poems are commonly tools of the Judgment, not of Imitation. By setting bounds to the imaging of Nature, these tools are to make the image that of one poet and not of another. At times Dryden took verse, rhyme, the unities to be such machine tools.

Judgment is indeed the Master-workman in a Play: but he requires many subordinate hands, many tools to his assistance. And Verse I affirm to be one of these.

And he was ready to throw away each tool when he found that it served not the whole Judgment but another gift. When he found that such a tool bounded the poet's sight of Nature not by the bounds of his own self, so as to become his own; but so that it was tied and belittled; he said so.

> He has now another taste of Wit;
> And, to confess a Truth (though out of Time,)
> Grows weary of his long-loved Mistris Rhyme.
> Passion 's too fierce to be in Fetters bound,
> And Nature flies him like Enchanted Ground.

In those who came after Dryden, these tools became the theory. There is no test of Correctness in Pope's *Essay on Criticism* which might not be quoted from Dryden. But the *Essay on Criticism* could not have been written by Dryden. For the *Essay on Criticism* is little more than the sum of these tests. Little is alive there but the tools; and after Pope, nothing else was alive for the Augustans. Where the great bases of the theory, Nature, Judgment, Wit were called on, they became merely tools. Dryden had pointed the way for the Augustans, when he had shirked speaking of his principles, and had been ready to take up and to drop one machine tool after another. Dryden was on the eve of the machine age of poetry. Only he held together the breaking world, the world of tools, which was to become that age.

3

I have said that Dryden's theory is the theory of a playwright. It is therefore just to study it in a play. And Dryden has chosen the play for us. At the end of his life, he wrote that he had written only one play for himself: *All for Love*. This is the play which I study.

In his Preface to *All for Love*, Dryden asks us to judge his play by the side of Shakespeare's *Antony and Cleopatra*. The names point to a difference between the plays. *Antony and Cleopatra* is a play about Antony and about Cleopatra. *All for Love, or The World Well Lost* is not about Cleopatra. She does not give all for love: all her being is love. She loses no world: her world is love, and she holds it. *All for Love* is a play about Antony.

This is the more striking, because Dryden's Cleopatra is a greater woman than Shakespeare's. Yet Dryden's rather than Shakespeare's Cleopatra betrays Antony. For Dryden's Cleopatra has a right to Antony's trust, and fails him. Shakespeare's Cleopatra is shifty and unworthy, but Antony understands her. Dryden's Cleopatra is altogether Antony's; but her forces are blind, and he cannot understand them. For Shakespeare's Antony is a man, and Dryden's is a god. Dryden's Antony is a god caught in the plans of men and women; and he is helpless, because he does not understand them.

This difference is everywhere in the plays. Dryden sets the tone of the heroic play in his first lines,

> Portents and Prodigies are grown so frequent
> That they have lost their Name.

The god and the everyday are already at grips; and *All for Love* is the story of their struggle. This is not the story which begins with Shakespeare's homely, lively lines,

> Nay, but this dotage of our Generals
> Ore-flowes the measure.

Antony and Cleopatra begins its story when Antony is first Cleopatra's lover. It tells of his going back to Rome, and of his marrying Octavia there in order to link himself with her brother Octavius. It tells of his falling back on Egypt when Octavius grows in power and grows threatening. And it tells of the sea-fight at Actium which first sounds Antony's doom, for he flies from it without a blow because Cleopatra has fled.

Only now, when nearly three acts of *Antony and Cleopatra* are done, do we reach the time of *All for Love*. And now it is plain that Antony is doomed. We meet him at the beginning of *All for Love* brooding and hopeless. The world has already beaten him. It is the world of Octavius and Cleopatra; for though they fight on opposing sides, they together beat him.

In *All for Love*, Antony is fighting against the world. Speaking of the forces against him, he says,

> *Octavius* is the Minion of blind Chance,
> But holds from Virtue nothing.

Blind chance is the image of the disorderly world, of

> Atoms casually together hurl'd,

which is always in Dryden's fears. Dryden has taken his cue from Shakespeare. Shakespeare's Antony has said of Octavius,

The very Dice obey him,
And in our sports my better cunning faints,
Vnder his chance, if we draw lots he speeds;

and has ruefully followed the image through the
lucks of gaming and cock-fighting. Shakespeare's
Antony is bewailing his luck because he is about to
fly to Egypt. This is not the mood of Dryden's Antony.
Dryden's Antony is at his moment of highest hope.
He is packing into the one image all that lies between
his mind and the mind of Octavius. He is marking
out the theme of the play, which sets against one
another the ideal Nature of Antony, and the world
by which he is beset.

In this theme, all who are against Antony are
symbols of the world. They are not only Octavius
and his Romans; but also the Egyptian court.
Antony's hopes are twice raised in *All for Love*, and
twice betrayed. Once they are betrayed by the
Egyptian fleet, which has already fled at Actium.
The fleet now rows out as if to fight Octavius; and
instead goes over to him. The second betrayal reaches
its head when the eunuch Alexas falsely tells Antony
that Cleopatra is dead. Egypt as surely as Rome
fights Antony, and Egypt fights more cunningly.

Their Soil and Heav'n infect 'em all with baseness,
And their young Souls come tainted to the World
With the first breath they draw.

The master of Egyptian betrayal is Cleopatra's eunuch
Alexas; its symbol is Cleopatra herself. Like Shakespeare, Dryden speaks of her as a snare and a toil.

8-2

She is the plainest of the worldly snares, the snare of the senses. Only because he falls into this snare is Antony overcome by Octavius.

Against these Antony is set, the hero and the god. He is the symbol of the ideal, which is beset by the worldly and which fights against it. At the beginning of the play, Antony has almost given up the fight. The forces of the world have worked together at Actium to humble him: Cleopatra has fled, and Octavius has won. Antony muses,

> I fancy
> I'm now turn'd wild, a Commoner of Nature;
> Of all forsaken, and forsaking all;
> Live in a shady Forrest's *Sylvan* Scene,
> Stretch'd at my length beneath some blasted Oke;
> I lean my head upon the Mossy Bark,
> And look just of a piece, as I grew from it:
> My uncomb'd Locks, matted like *Mistleto*,
> Hang o're my hoary Face; a murm'ring Brook
> Runs at my foot.

The silly thought puts us in mind of a hundred years of nymphs and shepherds, false Ardens and Arcadias, of Marie Antoinette in her dairy. Antony has sunk to the false nature of the court. But he does not belong to it; and he is broken out of it at once by Ventidius.

In *Antony and Cleopatra*, Antony's right hand man is Enobarbus, soldier, railer, and cynic. The well known praise of Cleopatra's state,

> The Barge she sat in, like a burnisht Throne
> Burnt on the water,

has an odd sharpness on his shrewd and shrewish
tongue. He is a man, who goes over to Octavius and
who dies for shame. Dryden's Antony has no such
gallant at his side. His right hand is Ventidius, not
a man but a soul, the soul of honour. To Dryden,
Antony is the ideal hero, and is the symbol of the
ideal Nature; and Ventidius is the tool of Nature
within man, the Judgment. When Ventidius tells
us what Antony is, he is telling us of the part he
himself plays to Antony.

> He censures eagerly his own misdeeds,
> Judging himself with malice to himself,
> And not forgiving what as Man he did,
> Because his other parts are more than Man.

And steadfastly Ventidius reminds Antony that
Antony is not a man but an ideal.

> You speak a Heroe, and you move a God,

he cries. Now he makes Antony look into his own
soul; and Antony is made himself again.

But the world still besets Antony. He is ashamed
and loth to leave Cleopatra. When he sends word
that he will not see her again,

> He seem'd not now that awful *Antony*,
> Who shook an Arm'd Assembly with his Nod;
> But making show as he would rub his eyes,
> Disguis'd and blotted out a falling tear.

Antony's tear is one of many which he weeps in
All for Love to mark the changes of his baffled heart.
Dryden has warned us in his prologue that Antony

> Weeps much; fights little; but is wond'rous kind.

Ventidius moves Antony with a tear; Octavia calls up another tear like that which Cleopatra caused,

> See how he winks! how he dries up a tear,
> That fain would fall!

The tears are weapons of the senses; they give way to fresh tears and fresh changes. Alexas the eunuch, the schemer of the senses, knows how to win back the kind Antony. He brings Antony a bracelet from Cleopatra which she must tie. In vain Ventidius, the Judgment, cries his warning,

> Touch not these poyson'd gifts,
> Infected by the sender, touch 'em not;
> Miriads of blewest Plagues lye underneath 'em,
> And more than Aconite has dipt the Silk.

Ventidius is using the fleshly image, to infect, which he uses of the Egyptian world,

> Their Soil and Heav'n infect 'em all with baseness.

We recall that Sidney spoke of the will infected by the senses. Cleopatra has infected Antony's will, and she has infected it by way of the senses. He takes her bracelet, and we know that he is lost. 'Y' are in the Toils' cries Ventidius.

Ventidius, the Judgment, has failed to bring back Antony. In despair, Ventidius tries to bring him back through others. He seeks out Antony's closest friend Dollabella. Dollabella is now with Octavius, where Antony has sent him because Dollabella fell in love with Cleopatra. Now Ventidius calls Dollabella, and with him Antony's wife Octavia and her children. Together they try to move Antony to leave Cleopatra and make peace with Octavius.

Dollabella is a puzzling symbol. I have likened Antony to Dryden's ideal Nature, and Ventidius to his Judgment. It is tempting to liken Dollabella to the Wit; and the likeness can be made in detail. But I do not want to press a donnish likeness. I am not looking for a likeness, but for Dollabella's place in Dryden's thought.

Dollabella is not of the world; like Ventidius, he is to draw Antony away from the world. But he is linked to the senses. In so far as he is linked to Antony also, he therefore betrays Antony. He is the man, whom Dryden's Nature cannot shake off. When Dollabella and Ventidius plead with Antony, they say,

Dollabella: Mine was an age when love might be excus'd,
　　When kindly warmth, and when my springing youth
　　Made it a debt to Nature. Yours—
Ventidius: Speak boldly.
　　Yours, he would say, in your declining age,
　　When no more heat was left but what you forc'd,
　　When all the sap was needful for the Trunk,
　　When it went down, then you constrain'd the course,
　　And robb'd from Nature, to supply desire.

The 'debt to Nature' is a debt to human nature. And Antony fails because his Nature, Dryden's Nature of the mind of man, cannot be rid of this debt. Dollabella and Ventidius may plead that the Nature which they make up must be free of the senses. They cannot hide that Dollabella takes his being from the

senses. This is Antony's thought when he sees Dollabella; he greets Dollabella with the images of marriage.

> Art thou return'd at last, my better half?
> Come, give me all myself.
> Let me not live,
> If the young Bridegroom, longing for his night,
> Was ever half so fond.

The image of the bridegroom has another irony.
Dryden has taken over the image from Shakespeare.
But in Shakespeare, the better half to which the
bridegroom Antony strains is death.

> I will bee
> A Bride-groome in my death, and run intoo't
> As to a Louers bed.

Dollabella is also Antony's death. He makes the
greatest betrayal, which dooms Antony. For when
Dollabella and Octavia have won over Antony a
second time, Antony sends Dollabella to bid Cleopatra
good-bye for him. Cleopatra's eunuch Alexas urges
her to be loving to Dollabella in order to make Antony
jealous. Dollabella also grows loving. Ventidius and
Octavia see them and tell Antony, in the hope that
he may find Cleopatra worthless. But all Antony's
feelings, even his jealousy, are swamped by a feeling
of bottomless betrayal.

> Heav'n should be ingenious
> In punishing such crimes. The rowling Stone
> And gnawing Vulture, were slight pains, invented
> When *Jove* was young, and no examples known
> Of mighty ills; but you have ripen'd sin
> To such a monstrous growth, 'twill pose the Gods
> To find an equal Torture. Two, two such.

He has been betrayed by the world; but he has also been betrayed by himself. His own better half has led him into the snare of the world. He no longer cares that Octavia goes back to her brother Octavius. He no longer cares that Cleopatra merely followed Alexas's scheme. He does not forgive Cleopatra because he does not forgive himself. When the Egyptian fleet betrays him, and Alexas heaps on the last betrayal of Cleopatra's death, he and Ventidius kill themselves. Nature and the soul's Judgment have lost. The world and the senses have won. All that is left alive of the soul is Dollabella. Dollabella has been to the soul as the Wit is: he has been the soul as it looks out on the senses, under the press of the senses. And his two-edged weapon has not saved the soul and Nature. In Dryden's image, Nature has fled from the world like Enchanted Ground.

4

I have set out the principles which make Dryden's theory of poetry. They are the principles of two worlds, which Dryden holds together. On one hand is the ideal; on the other the social world of man's senses. Sidney had believed that the social world could take its order from the ideal, in the fine moments of Virtue. Shelley came to believe that there was no ideal but a cleaner copy of the social world. Dryden does believe in an ideal. But even the name which he has for it, Nature, shows that it is an ideal which is not free of the natural world. It is founded in the world and in man. Yet it must be a greater Nature, because it must give order to the worldly nature. There is a telling line in *The Hind and the Panther* in which Dryden sets against one another the two natures. Dryden writes of the blasphemy of those who

Natures King through nature's opticks view'd.

He takes it for granted that we shall see that this is an evil thing to do. The eye belongs to the nature of the senses. But Christ is king of the ideal Nature, and to look on him as a natural man is plainly wrong. Nature's optics can give only a disorderly sight of the world. Nature's king has been sent to make it orderly.

To Dryden, the principle of order is the mind. There are three images which Dryden uses again and again in his poems. One is the image of the Enchanted Ground of Nature. The second is the image of the Lucretian atoms which chance rules; but which, for Dryden, a greater mind must order.

> From Harmony, from heav'nly Harmony
>   This universal Frame began;
> When Nature underneath a heap
>   Of jarring Atomes lay,
> And cou'd not heave her Head,
> The tuneful Voice was heard from high,
>   Arise, ye more than dead.

The third is the image of the ideal round. Dryden writes *Upon the Death of Oliver Cromwell*,

> How shall I then begin, or where conclude,
>   To draw a Fame so truly Circular?
> For in a Round, what Order can be shew'd,
>   Where all the Parts so equal perfect are?

And he packs the whole battle between senses and ideal into the line,

> Till rolling time is lost in round eternity.

This image of the restless balls coming to rest in the ideal round is linked to the image of the jarring atoms made orderly. And both are images of mind, and image an order of mind. In them speaks John Dryden, Fellow of the Royal Society; and we see in them that he is also John Dryden, Poet. To him the order of poetry, no less than the order of science, is an order of mind.

Dryden understands Nature as that root mind of man of which the mind of each man is a changed copy. It is the sum of those thoughts which all men share. But more than this, it is the principle of mind from which all common thoughts grow. This is the Nature which the poet imitates. In imitating it, the poet makes his own Nature. He makes it in two acts: an act of sense and an act of ordering. The first is the act of Wit, the second the act of Judgment. Both are acts of the mind, and so far orderly acts. But the Wit looks outward, and what it makes has the likeness of the outward nature, 'the Noble work of Chance'. The Judgment looks inward, and it shapes the making by the inward Nature, the round ideal.

The Wit and the Judgment alike are whole acts, and they are not set against Nature. The Augustans came to have a quarrel which still dulls our understanding of the word Nature: the quarrel, Nature against Art. In this quarrel, the Wit and the Judgment also took sides. Dryden does not share this quarrel. He uses it two or three times in his poems, as a formal piece of classicism.

> *Art* she had none, yet wanted none,
> For Nature did that Want supply.

But it is outside his thought, and is hardly glanced at in his essays. This is striking, in a writer who brought so many classical tests into English. Even Jonson made more of the quarrel than Dryden. After Dryden, it stood above other tests. But to Dryden it has no meaning. For to him Nature is an ideal of order; and the acts of man, Wit and Judgment, are acts towards this order. Only after Dryden died did poets see nature as the nature of the senses and of witty men, on which art must force an order of judgment.

Nevertheless, the change is foreshadowed in Dryden. For his Nature from which poets draw is a human nature. It is not the human nature to which Pope and Samuel Johnson were about to turn, and which was to become Shelley's god. But it is a step towards that social nature. It is a step away from Sidney's Virtue. Dryden no longer has Sidney's faith that the social life at moments can take its stamp from the ideal.

No Government has ever been, or ever can be, wherein Timeservers and Blockheads will not be uppermost. The Persons are only chang'd, but the same jugglings in State, the same Hypocrisie in Religion, the same Self-Interest, and Mis-mannagement, will remain for ever. Blood and Mony will be lavish'd in all Ages, only for the Preferment of new Faces, with old Consciences.

The word Virtue has grown dumb. Soon the Augustans were to break open this world cracked between the ideal and the social. The social world itself was to be made into a muddled kind of ideal. Dryden alone, with his bluff and stubborn strength, held the cracked world together. He alone for a moment upheld Antony against Octavius, the heroic Nature against the world. It was Shakespeare's Octavia who said of these two,

> Warres 'twixt you twaine would be,
> As if the world should cleaue, and that slaine men
> Should soader vp the Rift.

The wars had come, and the world had been cleft. For a few more years Dryden soldered up the rift. Dryden died, and Antony died; Octavius, Gaius Julius Caesar, became Augustus first emperor of Rome. The Augustan age had begun.

WORDSWORTH & COLERIDGE

WILLIAM WORDSWORTH

I

It is hard to think about Wordsworth and Coleridge without taking sides in the quarrel between them. It is the harder because this has become a quarrel not between two people but between two tempers. Two casts of feeling, two kinds of hope are set against one another. Worldly success is set against failure. These are our sides: and from them we find Wordsworth smug and Coleridge lively; or we find Wordsworth sterling and Coleridge shoddy.

And history has been just to Wordsworth and Coleridge. It has made theirs a quarrel between two psychological types because they chose to be psychologists. Wordsworth and Coleridge were pioneers of psychology. Above all, they first believed that poetry must be judged by the tests of psychology.

The Augustans had been the fathers of this belief. For the Augustans had made poetry a social act. In their time the social leaders had become the judges of poetry. And poetry in turn had become a judging of the social leaders: it had become satire. For a hundred years almost no poems had been written such as this book debates, whose end is outside the conduct of men. For a hundred years poets had sought the favour of men; and they had come to think this the only worth for which they might hope. At the end of the hundred years, in 1798, Wordsworth and Coleridge set out this belief as a theory of poetry.

They set it out in the Advertisement to the first edition of the *Lyrical Ballads*. This Advertisement does not yet make the clear charges against poetic writing which Wordsworth makes in the Preface to the second edition. But the gist of the charges is here. On this Wordsworth and Coleridge are at one: that poetry was then written in a stock manner on stock matters; and that it could become real only by changing manner and matter.

This is true; and readers eagerly ask, What is this real poetry to be? The answer is that it need not be poetry at all. Roundly the Advertisement tells its readers that they

should not suffer the solitary word Poetry, a word of very disputed meaning, to stand in the way of their gratification.

Why not? Because the *Lyrical Ballads* can give readers something which will gratify them as much as poetry.

They should ask themselves if it contains a natural delineation of human passions, human characters, and human incidents; and if the answer be favourable to the author's wishes, that they should consent to be pleased in spite of that most dreadful enemy to our pleasures, our own pre-established codes of decision.

This is a striking claim. The reader takes the *Lyrical Ballads* to be poems. He therefore judges them by his standard of poetry; and he may judge them to be bad. In answer, the Advertisement does not merely challenge his standard of poetry. It challenges the right of poetry to have any standard. It claims that if the *Lyrical Ballads* please a reader, this is all that can be asked of them. There is no standard for anything that is written or done. There is only the pleasure which these things give to this man or that.

The Advertisement to the *Lyrical Ballads* is short. But we see that its claim is far-reaching. Coleridge later implied that Wordsworth's Preface to the second edition of the *Lyrical Ballads* is a greater claim, reaching farther than Coleridge would follow. This is not so. Wordsworth's Preface is to set bounds to the boundless claim of the Advertisement. It is true that Coleridge disliked the bounds which Wordsworth set. But Coleridge no less than Wordsworth spent his life in hedging the claim of the Advertisement. My study is the hedges which each made.

Plainly the hedges had to be set round one word: pleasure. Some readers are pleased by that which does not please others. How are they to judge their different pleasures? By putting pleasures themselves in order of better and worse? But this is to put another standard in place of pleasure. By counting the men who share their pleasures? But this is to judge by the judgment of others. And the Advertisement is written exactly against this. It is written to ask each reader to judge alone, from his own pleasure.

No, the reader who is pleased by that which does not please others can only be told at last that he, the real he, is not pleased. Wordsworth puts this plainly in his Letter to John Wilson.

> Nothing is a fit subject for poetry which does not please. But here follows a question, Does not please whom?

> I answer, human nature as it has been [and ever] will be. But, where are we to find the best measure of this? I answer, [from with]in; by stripping our own hearts naked.

This is to take from the reader as much as was given him. He was told to please himself; and it turns out that he is to please that self which he would be if he were naked. More than this, he is given a model to which to strip. For Wordsworth goes on,

> by stripping our own hearts naked, and by looking out of ourselves to[wards men] who lead the simplest lives, and most according to nature.

With the words 'most according to nature', Wordsworth has denied the Advertisement. He has denied the standard of pleasure, and he has shifted his standard to nature: 'that is, to eternal nature, and the great moving spirit of things', he writes in the same letter. Wordsworth has gone back to standards which make pleasure merely an outcrop of poetic worth. He has put pleasure where Dryden put it when he wrote in his definition of wit,

> Pleasure follows of necessity, as the effect does the cause; and therefore is not to be put into the definition.

Wordsworth is hedging the word pleasure; and his hedges have left it almost no ground. The hedges make the careful form of his Preface to the second edition of the *Lyrical Ballads*. Here Wordsworth has put aside the Advertisement. No longer is the reader asked to let his pleasure guide him beyond 'the solitary word Poetry, a word of very disputed meaning'. No; at the outset the Preface tells him that in these poems only

that sort of pleasure and that quantity of pleasure may be imparted, which a Poet may rationally endeavour to impart.

Quietly the tables are turned. The reader whom pleasure was to guide beyond the word Poetry, is now to let the word Poet guide him to the right pleasure.

Wordsworth tells us what are the marks of the Poet on whom pleasure now hangs. I quote from his list that the poet is

a man pleased with his own passions and volitions, and who rejoices more than other men in the spirit of life that is in him; delighting to contemplate similar volitions and passions as manifested in the goings-on of the Universe, and habitually impelled to create them where he does not find them.

In these claims I read the core of Wordsworth's theory of poetry. The poet is pleased with his own passions: this pleasure is the model of all Wordsworth's pleasure. And he finds and makes like passions in the goings-on of the Universe. This is the model of the link with which Wordsworth bound his pleasure to the world of rivers and hills which filled his thought.

Dryden saw in poetry the ideal, root mind of man. Wordsworth sees in poetry the ideal, root passions of man. In these sits the poet's pleasure, to be 'pleased with his own passions and volitions'. From these the poet gives the only worthy pleasure, to please 'human nature as it has been [and ever] will be'. Wordsworth has found his bounds to pleasure in the root passions of man. To reach these the reader was asked to strip his heart naked. And his naked heart is Wordsworth's ideal of poetry. 'The Poet thinks and feels in the spirit of human passions.'

Only if we understand this shall we understand Wordsworth's Preface. The Preface is easily mistaken for an essay on prosody: how poems should be written, not what poetry is. Coleridge set the model for such mistakes when he attacked Wordsworth's claim to use 'a selection of language really used by men'. Wordsworth does make this claim at length, because he much dislikes 'the gaudiness and inane phraseology of many modern writers'. But he dislikes them because he dislikes the notion of poetry for which they stand. And in attacking them he is setting up another notion of poetry.

If the Poet's subject be judiciously chosen, it will naturally, and upon fit occasion, lead him to passions the language of which, if selected truly and judiciously, must necessarily be dignified and variegated, and alive with metaphors and figures.

In Wordsworth's notion good writing grows of itself from the passions; and grows from nothing else. Every hint for good writing and for good reading which Wordsworth gives is to graft the poem back on the root passions. Milton had claimed for poetry against rhetoric that it is more simple, sensuous, and passionate. We may read these as the three aims which Wordsworth sets himself in the *Lyrical Ballads*,

to choose incidents and situations from common life, and to relate or describe them, throughout, as far as was possible in a selection of language really used by men,

and, at the same time, to throw over them a certain colouring of imagination, whereby ordinary things should be presented to the mind in an unusual aspect;

and, further, and above all, to make these incidents and situations interesting by tracing in them, truly though not ostentatiously, the primary laws of our nature: chiefly, as far as regards the manner in which we associate ideas in a state of excitement.

But Wordsworth's aims are not three different aims. All three point to the third aim: to be passionate. I shall come to show how Wordsworth links his sensuous and imaginative feeling for nature to the passions. And he himself tells us how he links simpleness to the passions.

Humble and rustic life was generally chosen, because, in that condition, the essential passions of the heart find a better soil in which they can attain their maturity, are less under restraint, and speak a plainer and more emphatic language; because in that condition of life our elementary feelings coexist in a state of greater simplicity, and, consequently, may be more accurately contemplated, and more forcibly communicated; because the manners of rural life germinate from those elementary feelings, and, from the necessary character of rural occupations, are more easily comprehended, and are more durable; and, lastly, because in that condition the passions of men are incorporated with the beautiful and permanent forms of nature. The language, too, of these men has been adopted (purified indeed from what appear to be its real defects, from all lasting and rational causes of dislike or disgust) because such men hourly communicate with the best objects from which the best part of language is originally derived.

Each part of these sentences reaches back to the passions. In each Wordsworth makes the same claim: that he is simple the better to be passionate. I have quoted them at length for another reason. These are the sentences which Coleridge attacks in the *Biographia Literaria*.

Coleridge tells us that he attacks only one claim of Wordsworth: that poems should be written in the common speech. Part of his attack is just. For Wordsworth stretches this claim to say that poems should read like prose; and he can therefore give no good reason for writing them in verse. As Coleridge shows, Wordsworth here stretches his claim for simple poems too far. But it does not follow that Wordsworth stretches it too far whenever he makes it. Coleridge tries to show that he does. He tries to show that the simple feelings which Wordsworth seeks in humble and rustic life may be found as well or better in high and town life. Coleridge says that Wordsworth merely

judiciously laid the *scene* in the country, in order to place *himself* in the vicinity of interesting images, without the necessity of ascribing a sentimental perception of their beauty to the persons of his drama.

And Coleridge tries to show that humble and rustic speech is not more but less proper to poems; because it will not differ from the language of any other man of common-sense, however learned or refined he may be, except as far as the notions, which the rustic has to convey, are fewer and more indiscriminate. This will become still clearer, if we add the consideration (equally important though less obvious) that the rustic, from the more imperfect developement of his faculties, and from the lower state of their cultivation, aims almost solely to convey *insulated facts*, either those of his scanty experience or his traditional belief; while the educated man chiefly seeks to discover and express those *connections* of things, or those relative *bearings* of fact to fact, from which some more or less general law is deducible.

The best part of human language, properly so called, is derived from reflection on the acts of the mind itself.

Here stands the quarrel between Wordsworth and Coleridge. Plainly there are faults in Coleridge's wording of it. It is useless for Coleridge to say that a rustic's language will not differ from the language of any other man. In the year 1800, the speech of other men was as stilted as Wordsworth says. Nor does Coleridge make himself safe by hedging his other men to be 'of common-sense'. Wordsworth's claim is exactly that simple and country men were then almost the only men of common-sense. But we may overlook these faults. The quarrel stands: Granted that a simple, country speech is a speech of fact rather than of thought, is it therefore a better or worse speech for poems? And like the other quarrels of the Preface to the *Lyrical Ballads*, this is not a quarrel about speech but about poetry. It is a quarrel about the place of thought in Wordsworth's theory of poetry.

Wordsworth builds his theory of poetry on the passions or feelings. Yet Wordsworth's is a thoughtful poetry. If he believes that it rests on the feelings, it is because he believes that thought itself rests on the feelings.

All good poetry is the spontaneous overflow of powerful feelings: and though this be true, Poems to which any value can be attached were never produced on any variety of subjects but by a man who, being possessed of more than usual organic sensibility, had also thought long and deeply. For our continued influxes of feeling are modified and directed by our thoughts, which are indeed the representatives of all our past feelings.

These are Wordsworth's thoughts, 'the representatives of all our past feelings'; and their worth is that in turn they shape the feelings. And Wordsworth's claim is that such thought can be found best where feeling is best, in humble and rustic life. Coleridge may taunt the country man with 'the more imperfect developement of his faculties'. But which are the faculties which are ill developed in him? The thinking faculties, answers Coleridge: the faculties which 'seek to discover and express those *connections* of things' 'from which some more or less general law is deducible'. But Wordsworth cares nothing for such thinking and for these faculties. To him, poetry must indeed think. But it must think from the passions or feelings, and in order to begin new trains of feeling.

I have said that poetry is the spontaneous overflow of powerful feelings: it takes its origin from emotion recollected in tranquillity: the emotion is contemplated till, by a species of reaction, the tranquillity gradually disappears, and an emotion, kindred to that which was before the subject of contemplation, is gradually produced, and does itself actually exist in the mind.

This is Wordsworth's belief: that we think only after we feel, and that we think only the better to be able to feel. 'The Poet thinks and feels in the spirit of human passions.' For this reason Wordsworth has gone to humble and rustic life; and this is a reason which Coleridge has not overthrown.

The picture which I have quoted is striking for another reason. Set it by the side of Sidney's or of Dryden's picture of the poet at work: we are in a new world. Sidney, Jonson, Dryden cared about what the poet makes. Wordsworth cares about it; but he is torn by care about the poet's inward state. Wordsworth cares about psychology.

In this mood successful composition generally begins, and in a mood similar to this it is carried on; but the emotion, of whatever kind, and in whatever degree, from various causes, is qualified by various pleasures, so that in describing any passions whatsoever, which are voluntarily described, the mind will, upon the whole, be in a state of enjoyment.

Not the poet but the psychologist is speaking. And these are not rules of poetry, but tips for inward health. They are tips for making the most of pleasure.

2

The Advertisement to the *Lyrical Ballads* asks the reader to free himself from poetry and to look only for pleasure. Wordsworth's Preface to the *Lyrical Ballads* hedges this freedom by leading true pleasure back to the passions. The needs of poetry which the

Preface sets out are all to make it more passionate. But Wordsworth is still stubborn that the sum of these needs is the need to please.

Nor let this necessity of producing immediate pleasure be considered as a degradation of the Poet's art. It is far otherwise. It is an acknowledgement of the beauty of the universe, an acknowledgement the more sincere, because not formal, but indirect; it is a task light and easy to him who looks at the world in the spirit of love.

Wordsworth is marking a new place for pleasure. Pleasure makes man know the beauty of the universe. Pleasure is his love for the universe. Pleasure is man's link to the world.

I have quoted Wordsworth's search for this link. Wordsworth has pictured the poet as

a man pleased with his own passions and volitions, and who rejoices more than other men in the spirit of life that is in him; delighting to contemplate similar volitions and passions as manifested in the goings-on of the Universe, and habitually impelled to create them where he does not find them.

The poet links the man in himself to the world about himself, and the link is pleasure. And the man is the man of passion, the world is a world in which he finds and makes passion. Thus through pleasure passion has suddenly become a mover outside man. It has become the mover of the universe. Wordsworth is suddenly showing us a new and greater nature, not of the senses but of the passions. It is an ideal Nature which stands to the root passions of man as Dryden's ideal Nature stood to his root mind. And it is an ideal

Nature of which the natural world is merely the symbol. This is the ideal which makes poetry 'the image of man and nature' to Wordsworth. This is 'eternal nature, and the great moving spirit of things'.

This is the ideal to which Wordsworth's poems speak.

> Wisdom and Spirit of the universe!
> Thou Soul that art the eternity of thought!
> That giv'st to forms and images a breath
> And everlasting motion! not in vain,
> By day or star-light thus from my first dawn
> Of Childhood didst Thou intertwine for me
> The passions that build up our human Soul,
> Not with the mean and vulgar works of Man,
> But with high objects, with enduring things,
> With life and nature, purifying thus
> The elements of feeling and of thought,
> And sanctifying, by such discipline,
> Both pain and fear, until we recognize
> A grandeur in the beatings of the heart.

Within it, passion and the natural world are made one, held together by pleasure. Wordsworth has to hold them as one. Passion is his ideal; but the natural world is his master. The natural world gives the impulse and the images to his poems. It makes his memory: and there Wordsworth has known it at one with the passions. Wordsworth says this word for word:

> The sounding cataract
> Haunted me like a passion: the tall rock,
> The mountain, and the deep and gloomy wood,
> Their colours and their forms, were then to me
> An appetite; a feeling and a love.

Wordsworth's best poems go back to this oneness of the world and the passions. They find in this oneness the greater Nature, in which 'the passions of men are incorporated with the beautiful and permanent forms of nature'.

I study two of these poems, which Wordsworth has chosen himself. One is the *Lines Composed a Few Miles above Tintern Abbey* which Wordsworth put as his masterwork at the end of the *Lyrical Ballads*. The other is the *Ode: Intimations of Immortality from Recollections of Early Childhood* which he put as his masterwork at the end of his *Poems*.

Tintern Abbey already looks back for the oneness of the world and the passions. Its theme is the change in Wordsworth since he came to Tintern Abbey five years before. Now as then the scene is beautiful to him, and he pictures it lovingly. And it has been beautiful to him throughout the five years. In remembering it he has been less tired and more happy in his life in towns: and therefore he has been more kind to men. And the memory has also made a deeper mood, of understanding the great moving Nature. I give the picture of the two moods in Wordsworth's two sentences.

> Sensations sweet,
> Felt in the blood, and felt along the heart;
> And passing even into my purer mind,
> With tranquil restoration:—feelings too
> Of unremembered pleasure: such, perhaps,
> As have no slight or trivial influence
> On that best portion of a good man's life,

His little, nameless, unremembered, acts
Of kindness and of love.
      Nor less, I trust,
To them I may have owed another gift,
Of aspect more sublime; that blessed mood,
In which the burthen of the mystery,
In which the heavy and the weary weight
Of all this unintelligible world,
Is lightened:—that serene and blessed mood,
In which the affections gently lead us on,—
Until, the breath of this corporeal frame
And even the motion of our human blood
Almost suspended, we are laid asleep
In body, and become a living soul:
While with an eye made quiet by the power
Of harmony, and the deep power of joy,
We see into the life of things.

Wordsworth hopes that he is now storing food for these moods as he stored it then, although he is not what he was then. There follow the lines which I have quoted, which tell how wholly passion and the natural world were at one in him then. He has lost this oneness. He feels that he has found two things in its stead. He has found that the natural scene can now make him think kindly of humanity. And he has found a mood of understanding the great Nature. Again I give the picture of the two moods in Wordsworth's two sentences.

      I have learned
To look on nature, not as in the hour
Of thoughtless youth; but hearing oftentimes
The still, sad music of humanity,
Nor harsh nor grating, though of ample power
To chasten and subdue.

> And I have felt
> A presence that disturbs me with the joy
> Of elevated thoughts; a sense sublime
> Of something far more deeply interfused,
> Whose dwelling is the light of setting suns,
> And the round ocean and the living air,
> And the blue sky, and in the mind of man:
> A motion and a spirit, that impels
> All thinking things, all objects of all thought,
> And rolls through all things.

Here the theme of *Tintern Abbey* ends. It is merely traced again in the life which Wordsworth foretells for Dorothy Wordsworth.

The theme is striking for its pictures of two moods. In town Wordsworth drew two moods from the memory of his passionate sight of nature: kindness to men, and faith that the world is moved by a greater mover. These are the very moods which he now draws from the sight of nature itself: a kindness to mankind, and faith that the world is moved by a greater Nature. When Wordsworth sees the Wye now he feels only what he used to feel when he remembered seeing the Wye. Thus Wordsworth's feeling for nature has wholly changed: it has become a feeling at a remove. I recall that for Wordsworth poetry grows from emotion recollected in tranquillity. To write poems he must therefore have emotions, in order that he may recollect them. But Wordsworth's moods at the Wye are no longer emotions. Strikingly they follow those recollections of earlier emotions which he himself tells. And they can serve only as recollections. In spite of his bluster

That I, so long
A worshipper of Nature, hither came
Unwearied in that service: rather say
With warmer love,

in spite of his hope

That in this moment there is life and food
For future years,

he knows that there is no love and no life. And Wordsworth came to write such loveless, lifeless poems because he would stubbornly recollect these moments. He was recollecting recollections, not emotions; and therefore his poems became the moral memoirs of a retired poet.

I stress this because I think that *Tintern Abbey* is a turning point in Wordsworth's writing. I think that in *Tintern Abbey* Wordsworth is trying to make up his mind to give up the failing impulse of the natural scene, and to find another impulse for his poems. The doubts which fill *Tintern Abbey* show that Wordsworth was ready to close one part of his poetic life with it, as he closed the *Lyrical Ballads* with it. For plainly *Tintern Abbey* and *The Prelude* are meant to sum a life; and Wordsworth might have turned to a new life. Unhappily *Tintern Abbey* and *The Prelude* turned out to be better than any poems which Wordsworth had written. They tempted him to draw out the very life which they were to close. Moreover, Wordsworth felt the failure of the impulse of nature as his own failure. His steady feeling of guilt therefore held him in the life of nature, and stifled his poetry.

For Wordsworth's poetry failed at last because he would still begin and end it in the natural scene. There he still sought his impulse and there he sought his images. He still wrote in the tight circle of *Tintern Abbey*. His poetry failed because any poetry so self-enclosed must fail. There is no movement from impulse to image, and from image to impulse. There is no movement from thought to feeling, and from feeling to thought, such as Wordsworth himself asks for,

Our continued influxes of feeling are modified and directed by our thoughts, which are indeed the representatives of all our past feelings.

There is no forward movement, only the round movement within one world. Such poems can only double back on themselves without end. *Tintern Abbey* shows this clearly. Thought and image turn back and back on themselves: scene, memory of scene, memory of how the scene was seen, hope how the scene will be remembered, in an endless knot. There is no going forward from here. It ends in the tied beauty of

> A sense sublime
> Of something far more deeply interfused,
> Whose dwelling is the light of setting suns,
> And the round ocean and the living air,
> And the blue sky, and in the mind of man:
> A motion and a spirit, that impels
> All thinking things, all objects of all thought,
> And rolls through all things.

This is an unequalled picture of choking yet uplifting helplessness in the face of great beauty of scene. But it is also a Gordian knot of the feelings, from which the poem cannot cut free. In it the natural scene is forward impulse, backward image, and is the link through which they play.

Many reasons have been given for the decay of Wordsworth's poems: a handful of silver, the quarrel with Coleridge, the forsaking of a lover and child. No doubt each has something of the truth. Each tells something of the feeling of guilt and failure which runs under Wordsworth's poems. Each is a shadow of the same weakness. But the weakness lies deeper than the reasons. It is a weakness within Wordsworth's thought. His thought is closed within the natural world. Even his ideal Nature of passion drives him back on this world. For Wordsworth has once taken his passion from this world. Therefore every passion takes him back to it. Every passion makes him mourn a lost world and a lost youth.

This is the theme of the *Ode: Intimations of Immortality from Recollections of Early Childhood*. The poem begins with the complaint of *Tintern Abbey*: that Wordsworth is no longer moved by the natural world as he used to be. But now Wordsworth tells us that he is not alone in being unmoved. All men are less moved as they grow older, because to be moved by nature is the gift of youth. Wordsworth here draws a remarkable picture of man. It begins at the Platonic picture, to which Wordsworth points in a note to Miss Fenwick. Like Plato, Wordsworth believes that the soul at birth has already known all that it slowly uncovers in its life.

> Our birth is but a sleep and a forgetting:
> The Soul that rises with us, our life's Star,
>   Hath had elsewhere its setting,
>   And cometh from afar.

This is good Plato, and Wordsworth makes it fair Christianity.

>   Not in entire forgetfulness,
>   And not in utter nakedness,
> But trailing clouds of glory do we come
> From God, who is our home.

But these quiet words hide a meaning which has nothing of Plato in it. 'Not in entire forgetfulness' is suddenly to turn the Platonic belief upside down. For Plato held that the soul forgets its knowledge at birth, and that life is a remembering piece by piece of this knowledge. Wordsworth's soul remembers its knowledge at birth, but its life is a forgetting of it piece by piece.

> Shades of the prison-house begin to close
>   Upon the growing Boy,
> But he beholds the light, and whence it flows,
>   He sees it in his joy;
> The Youth, who daily farther from the east
>   Must travel, still is Nature's Priest,
>   And by the vision splendid
>   Is on his way attended;
> At length the Man perceives it die away,
> And fade into the light of common day.

This is not an actual picture. No doubt many men feel in youth a oneness with rivers and hills which they lose later; as Wordsworth did. But it is not likely that they have brought this feeling from childhood; still less that the feeling was deeper in childhood. Wordsworth's picture of the child here is as fanciful as Coleridge showed it to be.

Wordsworth's picture can be true only if we see it like Plato's as the symbol of an ideal. Wordsworth is picturing a singleness and a whole knowledge which man never reaches because they belong to the soul. His child is the symbol of the soul, which brings to the world an ideal knowledge which is not of the world. The knowledge is passionate oneness with the natural scene.

This oneness had been the core of *Tintern Abbey*. But there it had been a knowledge in the senses. The *Intimations of Immortality* first plainly makes it a knowledge of the soul. It plainly makes the natural world the symbol of ideal Nature: and it is Wordsworth's clearest avowal of his belief in ideal Nature. Unhappily it is all the more a hopeless poem. *Tintern Abbey* had been ready to give up the natural scene, which moved Wordsworth less and less. The *Intimations of Immortality* no longer hopes to break from the natural scene. It pleads that Wordsworth's failure to be moved is the failure of all men. It builds a careful and remarkable Platonism-upside-down to uphold this plea. The oneness of passion and nature is an ideal of the soul before birth, says Wordsworth; and after birth the soul must slowly lose it. The child still holds it; the youth can recall it; the man yearns back to it and to all the thoughts which the child had from it,

> Those first affections,
> Those shadowy recollections,

> Which, be they what they may,
> Are yet the fountain-light of all our day,
> Are yet a master-light of all our seeing;
>   Uphold us, cherish, and have power to make
> Our noisy years seem moments in the being
> Of the eternal Silence.

Wordsworth will not give up the natural world. And now he sees in it all that man can hold to and must search back for. He has grown content to find in it the two moods of kindliness and uplift of *Tintern Abbey*, and he writes,

> Though nothing can bring back the hour
> Of splendour in the grass, of glory in the flower;
>   We will grieve not, rather find
>   Strength in what remains behind;
>   In the primal sympathy
>   Which having been must ever be;
>   In the soothing thoughts that spring
>   Out of human suffering;
>   In the faith that looks through death,
> In years that bring the philosophic mind.

It is the end of Wordsworth's poetic life. From now on the symbol in the natural world gives place to the fact, and the fact to the moral. The Sky-lark of 1805 straining for 'higher raptures' becomes the Skylark of 1825,

> Type of the wise who soar, but never roam;
> True to the kindred points of Heaven and Home!

Both are Wordsworth closed in the round of the natural world. At the end of the *Intimations of Immortality* Wordsworth fiercely claims that still

To me the meanest flower that blows can give
Thoughts that do often lie too deep for tears.

He now spent his life in making an endless chain of
such moral flower pieces.

3

I have pictured Wordsworth as a divided man. His
theory of poetry is a divided theory. The *Intimations
of Immortality* shows that it is a theory of the soul. But
the twisted Platonism shows even here, as *Tintern
Abbey* shows, that it is also a theory of the senses.
Wordsworth tried to hold the two together within
the natural scene. And Wordsworth failed.

To Wordsworth, poetry is a mode of the ideal
Nature which moves man and the world. This Nature
is the root passions of man. Wordsworth's Preface to
the *Lyrical Ballads* sets out this ideal: poetry must
speak from the root passions, and these passions must
be made one with the natural world. All the rules
of the Preface lead back to the passions. And Wordsworth will not break them up for the passions of
this man or that. He seeks the passions common to
all men; and more, the root passions from which all
passion springs. He finds them in the passion which
the natural world has once moved in him.

Now it is manifest that no human being can be so
besotted and debased by oppression, penury, or any other
evil which unhumanizes man, as to be utterly insensible
to the colours, forms, or smell of flowers, the [voices]
and motions of birds and beasts, the appearances of the
sky and heavenly bodies.

Wordsworth links passion to the natural world by pleasure: because he stubbornly believes that pleasure must be the same in all men. When he asks the first readers of the *Lyrical Ballads* to follow only their pleasure, he does believe that they cannot be taking pleasure in the poems which he dislikes. He cannot believe that some readers like stilted poems; and only slowly can he bring himself to hedge their pleasure, to set right their taste, and to make the taste for his own poems. Above all he cannot believe that anyone does not take pleasure in the natural world. Therefore the natural world is the symbol of ideal Nature, and is also the true mover of the passions. The soul hangs on the natural scene. The key to Wordsworth's thought here is the claim,

> Nor let this necessity of producing immediate pleasure be considered as a degradation of the Poet's art. It is far otherwise. It is an acknowledgement of the beauty of the universe.

In thus setting the soul under the natural world, Wordsworth is building on a contradiction. He is drawing from the world of the body the mood in which

> We are laid asleep
> In body, and become a living soul.

Therefore he judges the wakefulness of the soul by the body's readiness to be moved by nature. This contradicting standard makes the oddities and cross-purposes of *Tintern Abbey* and the *Intimations of Immortality*. It makes the guilt and hopelessness, the outcast mood, and the decay of Wordsworth's poems. For by this standard Wordsworth finds himself wanting.

Some have found a reason for Wordsworth's decay in the quarrel with Coleridge. But Wordsworth's decay grows from the contradiction of judging the soul by the pleasure of the senses. Therefore it grows from the beliefs which Wordsworth shared with Coleridge; not from those on which they quarrelled. For Coleridge did found poetry in pleasure. Coleridge began the pleasure psychology which has taken the place of the criticism of poetry for a hundred years. Wordsworth has taken up pleasure psychology almost by mistake; and it is his undoing. For Wordsworth is the last of the line of poets which runs through Sidney, Jonson, and Dryden. Wordsworth holds an ideal of poetry which is almost religious: he himself points its likeness to religion in the *Essay, Supplementary to the Preface*. Coleridge is one of the first in the line of social poets which runs through Shelley, Swinburne, and their heirs. And Wordsworth failed because he could not keep his thought free from the social and psychological thought of these poets.

Wordsworth allowed the belief in pleasure to enclose him in the natural scene. He drew his impulse and feelings from the natural scene; and he also drew his images and thoughts from the natural scene. His failure is not caused by the natural scene; it is not caused by this or any other field. It is caused by the tight round in which any such field encloses a poet. Wordsworth lost the gift to be moved by the images of the poem to fresh impulses, and by the impulses to fresh images. This is a common loss. We do not commonly feel it because we find new impulses in the images which our first impulses have called up. We move forward turn by turn. Wordsworth decayed because this movement went round and round in a treadmill. His trains of thought came back on themselves. His images no longer moved forward and no longer moved him. They were the images of the world of which he had said,

Now it is manifest that no human being can be so besotted and debased by oppression, penury, or any other evil which unhumanizes man, as to be utterly insensible to the colours, forms, or smell of flowers, the [voices] and motions of birds and beasts, the appearances of the sky and heavenly bodies.

Besotted and debased: the bitter words tell us how bitterly Wordsworth felt his failure to take pleasure in the natural world. For Wordsworth judged the soul by the pleasure of the senses. In that judgment the soul had already failed.

SAMUEL TAYLOR COLERIDGE

I

WORDSWORTH wrote *Tintern Abbey* in 1798 and finished the *Intimations of Immortality* in 1806. In 1802 Coleridge wrote *Dejection: An Ode*. The three poems are steps in a debate whose fourth step was the quarrel between Wordsworth and Coleridge. For the three poems made plain that Wordsworth and Coleridge at last had no common ground. And the poems point their difference more plainly than any other of Wordsworth's and Coleridge's writings.

At the beginning of *Dejection* Coleridge sees the New-moon with the old Moon in her lap. He recalls the ballad, and writes,

> Well! If the Bard was weather-wise, who made
> The grand old ballad of Sir Patrick Spence,
> This night, so tranquil now, will not go hence
> Unroused by winds.

The homely ease and humour of these lines is Coleridge's nicest gift. Alas, he drops it at once. He reads the signs of storm, and now he finds his stage voice,

> And oh! that even now the gust were swelling,
> And the slant night-shower driving loud and fast!
> Those sounds which oft have raised me, whilst they awed,
> And sent my soul abroad,
> Might now perhaps their wonted impulse give,
> Might startle this dull pain, and make it move and live!

Coleridge grieves that nature no longer gives its wonted impulse. This was Wordsworth's grief in *Tintern Abbey*, and Coleridge is frank that he has taken it from Wordsworth. The first draft of *Dejection* was written to Sara Hutchinson; but it and later drafts spoke to Wordsworth by name, and only after the quarrel did Coleridge change these *O Williams* and *O Wordsworths* to *O Lady*. Coleridge was answering Wordsworth on his own ground.

But the nature which fails Coleridge is not the nature of Wordsworth. Not gusts and slant night-showers had moved Wordsworth, and *Tintern Abbey* does not mourn their loss. *Tintern Abbey* is the poem of a man who is alive to the common happenings of the country,

> These hedge-rows, hardly hedge-rows, little lines
> Of sportive wood run wild: these pastoral farms,
> Green to the very door; and wreaths of smoke
> Sent up, in silence, from among the trees.

It mourns the loss of the poet's passionate oneness with these common happenings. *Dejection* is the poem of a man who seeks only the thunder and display of the country. Coleridge has lost no passionate impulse, but his interest in the theatre of nature: gust and slant night-shower, green light that lingers in the west, the Actor wind,

> Thou Actor, perfect in all tragic sounds!
> Thou Wind, that rav'st without,
>   Bare crag, or mountain-tairn, or blasted tree,
> Or pine-grove whither woodman never clomb,
> Or lonely house, long held the witches' home.

Coleridge's nature is not Wordsworth's but a nature of show; and Coleridge's loss is not Wordsworth's loss.

To Wordsworth, the loss of his passionate oneness with the natural world was the loss of his life. This was the root, and every other loss, every guilt and failure grew from it. Coleridge's loss of interest in the storms and shows of nature is merely one sign of the aimless and bored grief which has overtaken him,

> A grief without a pang, void, dark, and drear,
> A stifled, drowsy, unimpassioned grief,
> Which finds no natural outlet, no relief,
>   In word, or sigh, or tear.

Listless, hopeless: it is the picture of Coleridge in these years, as Dorothy Wordsworth catches it in her *Journals*. No romantic sight of nature will move his passion,

> I see them all so excellently fair,
> I see, not feel, how beautiful they are;

because no sight of nature has made his passion. Coleridge writes,

> I may not hope from outward forms to win
> The passion and the life, whose fountains are within.

This sentence is true because Coleridge writes it of himself. It has the psychological insight which is a gift and a discovery of Coleridge, and which he does not often turn on himself. Coleridge is right: he cannot hope to make himself well by looking at the natural world, because his sickness does not come from the natural world. His sickness is within, as all Coleridge's life is within himself. Coleridge is right to write of himself the lines which are the core of *Dejection*,

> O Lady! we receive but what we give,
> And in our life alone does Nature live:
> Ours is her wedding garment, ours her shroud!
>   And would we aught behold, of higher worth,
> Than that inanimate cold world allowed
> To the poor loveless ever-anxious crowd,
>   Ah! from the soul itself must issue forth
> A light, a glory.

The fault of these lines is that they are written to Wordsworth.

The lines understand Coleridge's sight of nature: they wholly misunderstand Wordsworth's sight of nature. 'Ours is her wedding garment, ours her shroud' attacks a romantic view of nature. But Wordsworth did not think of nature as romantic, even at his wedding, for which *Dejection* was a present. Only to Coleridge is nature a romance of wedding garments and shrouds. Only Coleridge

judiciously laid the *scene* in the country, in order to place *himself* in the vicinity of interesting images.

And only Coleridge could believe that this is what Wordsworth did.

Wordsworth answers all this part of *Dejection* in the *Intimations of Immortality*. I think that *Intimations of Immortality* is a wrong-headed poem, with which Wordsworth gives up hope of beginning a new poetic life. But Wordsworth does understand there what is the Nature which he seeks. He does hold there an ideal of passion greater than his own passions. He sees the natural world as the symbol of this ideal. He sees the loss of his passionate oneness with the natural world as symbol of the loss of an ideal. Wordsworth understands that the loss is not in himself. Ideal Nature has given him up, and he will never be a poet again. When Wordsworth made this answer he knew that he had nothing in common with Coleridge.

His fault was that he held to one belief of Coleridge: the belief in pleasure. This is the belief which *Dejection* must reach. What have I lost? asks Coleridge; and answers,

> Joy, virtuous Lady! Joy that ne'er was given,
>   Save to the pure, and in their purest hour,
>   Life, and Life's effluence, cloud at once and shower,
>   Joy, Lady! is the spirit and the power,
> Which wedding Nature to us gives in dower
>   A new Earth and new Heaven,
>   Undreamt of by the sensual and the proud—
> Joy is the sweet voice, Joy the luminous cloud—
>   We in ourselves rejoice!

This is apt to Coleridge. Pleasure is the core of the psychology which he founded. Wordsworth takes over pleasure; but again Wordsworth's is not Coleridge's pleasure. Wordsworth's pleasure is the tool with which the natural world moves the passions. Coleridge's pleasure is the business of man with himself,

> We in ourselves rejoice;

when it reaches nature, it is pleasure which man takes in the self which he has put into nature. Coleridge

tells us that once no mishap could damp his pleasure.
But now,

> But now afflictions bow me down to earth:
> Nor care I that they rob me of my mirth;
>   But oh! each visitation
> Suspends what nature gave me at my birth,
>   My shaping spirit of Imagination.
> For not to think of what I needs must feel,
>   But to be still and patient, all I can;
> And haply by abstruse research to steal
>   From my own nature all the natural man—
>   This was my sole resource, my only plan:
> Till that which suits a part infects the whole,
> And now is almost grown the habit of my soul.

The lines tell us that Coleridge reads in his loss of
pleasure a loss of Imagination. And they tell us that
this loss has made Coleridge a thinker. The two points
are the last of *Dejection*, which now ends in a scene
of storm and fine wishes. The points are worth following beyond the scene.

I follow the second point. A year before he wrote
Dejection Coleridge wrote to Humphry Davy of what
he wanted to do. He wanted to write a book about

the affinities of the feelings with words and ideas under
the title of "Concerning Poetry, and the nature of the
Pleasures derived from it". I have faith that I do understand the subject, and I am sure that if I write what
I ought to do on it, the work would supersede all the
books of metaphysics, and all the books of morals too.

It does not strike Coleridge that a book to supersede
the books of metaphysics and morals goes oddly by
the name *Concerning Poetry*. Certainly he does not
think it odd that *Concerning Poetry* should really be

about 'the affinities of the feelings with words and ideas'. For Coleridge is not interested in poetry. Poetry is the field of his study, only because it is a good field for experiments in metaphysics, morals, and the feelings. These are the ends of his study. They are ends within Coleridge's only lasting interest: pleasure psychology. Therefore Coleridge studies them in the nature of the pleasures derived from poetry. He is not studying poetry but the psychology of those who like poetry. He wrote of a like scheme to Southey,

The object is not to examine what is good in each writer, but what has *ipso facto* pleased, and to what faculties, or passions, or habits of the mind they may be supposed to have given pleasure.

Coleridge himself does not think his study the best or the right study of poetry. I have quoted the lines from *Dejection*,

By abstruse research to steal
From my own nature all the natural man—
This was my sole resource, my only plan:
Till that which suits a part infects the whole,
And now is almost grown the habit of my soul.

Coleridge is excusing his act of leaving poetry for metaphysics. But the excuse is not for one act: it is for the change of Coleridge's interest within every act. When Coleridge allows that abstruse research is almost grown the habit of his soul, he allows that his interest in all matters has become a scientific and social interest. His excuse tells us that he does not think this the best or the right interest.

The sentences which Coleridge wrote to Davy are therefore apt to *Dejection*. Their interest, like that of *Dejection*, is not in poetry. The interest of both is in pleasure and pleasure psychology. In both Coleridge believes that pleasure is the key to every question which man asks.

Wordsworth shared Coleridge's belief in pleasure. In the Advertisement to the *Lyrical Ballads*, Wordsworth had also put pleasure in place of poetry. Wordsworth had not been able to hold it there; and he had gone back to find an ideal in poetry. When Wordsworth grieves in *Tintern Abbey* that river and hill no longer move him as they did, he mourns the loss of an ideal Nature of which he is the mouthpiece. When Coleridge writes of a like grief in a like way in *Dejection*, he mourns his loss of interest in the stage display of a hilly country. He feels that this interest has been like an interest in the soul, and that his new interest in abstruse research is not equal to it. But the change of interest is only a loss within Coleridge. For the natural world only gave Coleridge pleasure in himself. This is the pleasure which he seeks everywhere, and which he always seeks to understand. It is not Wordsworth's pleasure, and Wordsworth denies it once for all in the *Intimations of Immortality*. Wordsworth does not believe, as Coleridge believes, that man answers every question when he understands the pleasures which he takes in himself. The study of these pleasures was Coleridge's step in psychology. In making it, Coleridge did able and pioneer work in this social science. He did as able pioneer work in seeing that poetry was a good field for experiments in this science. His pupils such as I. A. Richards are right to praise this work. But his work tells us nothing of what poetry is itself. His pupils have mistaken it for work within poetry itself. Coleridge himself does not mistake it and does not claim this for it. He does not claim for it more than the name of an abstruse research. He knows that he is looking, not into that soul which he calls the natural man, but into the social conduct of men. Coleridge holds that pleasure is the key to metaphysics and morals and conduct. At his best he does not hold that it is the key to poetry.

2

Coleridge studies poetry by way of pleasure. When he has lectured on some lesser things which must be in a poem, he tells us what must be there above all.

No work could deserve the title of poem which did not include those circumstances—but *together with something else*.

What then is this something? With much diffidence, he would answer that

It is that pleasurable emotion, that peculiar state and degree of excitement that arises in the poet himself in the act of composition.

And in order to understand this we must combine under the notion of true poet more than ordinary sensibility, occasioning a more than ordinary sympathy with the objects of nature or the incidents of human life.

The picture of the poet might be taken from Wordsworth's Preface to the *Lyrical Ballads*; and no doubt Coleridge is remembering the Preface. But Coleridge always sees the poem in the same way.

I will venture to give the following definition of poetry.
It is an art (or whatever better term our language may afford) of representing, in words, external nature and human thoughts and affections, both relatively to human affections, by the production of as much immediate pleasure in parts, as is compatible with the largest sum of pleasure in the whole.

I single out the words which carry another echo of Wordsworth, and which are in both quotations: 'the objects of nature or the incidents of human life', 'external nature and human thoughts and affections'. Wordsworth had coupled the two, and had found in Nature the symbol of the passions. Why does Coleridge also couple them? Why does Coleridge speak of the natural scene at all when he speaks of poetry? Why does he write to Sotheby,

A poet's heart and intellect should be *combined*, intimately combined and unified with the great appearances of nature?

No doubt there are more reasons than one. One reason is that Coleridge follows Wordsworth's thought. Another is that Coleridge at all times wants to make a scheme of the world, and such a scheme must find a place for the natural scene. Above these is another reason. Coleridge's memory links the natural scene to the time when he and Wordsworth were writing the *Lyrical Ballads*. This was the time of his best poems, whose passing he mourns in *Dejection*. Coleridge lost this time together with his interest in the natural scene; and therefore when he looks back wistfully to poetry, he couples it with the natural scene.

These and other reasons tell why Coleridge makes the love of nature a part of the make-up of poets. I have said that Coleridge's nature is not Wordsworth's. Coleridge's poet does not take his impulse from nature. He merely 'places *himself* in the vicinity of interesting images'. And at last it is he who makes the images interesting and alive.

> O Lady! we receive but what we give,
> And in our life alone does Nature live.

We must see to what lengths Coleridge takes this belief.

Lecturing on Aristotle's Imitation of Nature, Coleridge says,

This leads us to what the drama should be. And first it is not *a copy* of nature; but it is an imitation. This is the universal principle of the fine arts. In every well-laid out grounds, what delight do we feel from that balance and antithesis of feelings and thought. "How natural!" we say; but the very wonder that furnished the *how* implies that we perceived art at the same moment. We catch the hint from nature itself. Whenever in mountains or cataracts we discover a likeness to anything artificial which we yet know was not artificial, what pleasure! So in appearances known to be artificial that appear natural.

This is surely a staggering claim of the pleasure judgment. Coleridge takes pleasure in a garden because it is not nature. It is like nature, but it is also a little unlike; and from the little unlikeness spring Coleridge's pleasure and his judgment of worth. Thus the garden is worthy because it betrays the living maker, and only in that which betrays the living maker. And Coleridge takes the oddity a step farther.

We catch the hint from nature itself. Whenever in mountains or cataracts we discover a likeness to anything artificial which we yet know was not artificial, what pleasure!

This tells us as plainly as *Dejection* what interest Coleridge takes in nature. Nature pleases him because it carries a hint of man's art. Wordsworth would have been shocked to hear Coleridge grant this, that he goes to mountains or cataracts because he discovers a likeness to something artificial. It is blunt but not shocking. This is Coleridge's belief: that the natural scene is worthy only as it is filled by the life of man.

Wordsworth knew the *Influence of Natural Objects in Calling Forth and Strengthening the Imagination.* Coleridge does not know this influence. He knows only the influence of the imagination in calling forth the life of natural objects. The only worth which he allows is the instant living spark with which the poet fires the world with feeling. Coleridge likes to find its model in Shakespeare's tragic puns. In these puns some trapped and baffled mind spills all its bitterness: Hamlet, Gaunt; the deposed Richard II, 'Being so great, I haue no neede to begge', Laertes, 'Too much of water hast thou poore *Ophelia*'. Coleridge reads in these puns the natural tendency of the mind immersed in one strong feeling to connect that feeling with every sight and object around it.

This has psychological insight. It is also the model of Coleridge's Imagination.

Like Wordsworth, Coleridge sets a link between man and the natural objects. Like Wordsworth's, Coleridge's link is pleasure. But Coleridge's link springs from man to the objects. The object of the pun is apt and springs back upon the mind only because the mind's passion has made it apt. It pleases, it moves the feelings only because it has been charged with feeling. The natural scene is looped back upon the feelings and takes its realness from them:

the natural tendency of the mind immersed in one strong feeling to connect that feeling with every sight and object around it.

The punster strikes a flash of life from the scene, and it is his own life.

Coleridge's link is made to give life to the natural scene. And Coleridge makes it the simplest link which can do this. He simply makes it the power by which man gives his own life to the natural objects. Coleridge calls this power Imagination.

Coleridge's theory of Imagination has been understood in many ways by many men. There is no doubt what Coleridge means, roughly. Roughly, Coleridge believes that there is an act of the mind which is so much more full and lively than any other that it is different in kind. Coleridge calls this act Imagination.

But between this 'roughly' and the understanding of Coleridge's theory lie deeper questions. Why must the Imagination be in Coleridge's scheme? What must it do there? Only when we answer these questions do we understand Coleridge. The difference between understanding roughly and understanding Coleridge is a difference in kind.

Coleridge's theory of Imagination grows from his study of man in the face of the natural objects. In this it is the heir of his friendship with Wordsworth and of the spurt of poems which this friendship struck from both. It is the heir of the debate which I have read from *Tintern Abbey* to *Dejection* and from *Dejection* to the *Intimations of Immortality*. It is the putting into a theory of the cry of faith from *Dejection*,

> O Lady! we receive but what we give,
> And in our life alone does Nature live.

It is the claim which runs under everything which Coleridge writes, about gardens or about puns: that man's worth is to be alive, and that all else gains worth only by partaking in his act of being alive.

Thus the theory of Imagination takes up both the themes of *Dejection*. Like *Dejection* it grows from Coleridge's belief that pleasure in the natural scene is the need of poets. I recall that Coleridge has read in his loss of this pleasure a loss of Imagination,

> But oh! each visitation
> Suspends what nature gave me at my birth,
> My shaping spirit of Imagination.

And like *Dejection* the theory of Imagination sees this pleasure as the life of nature and sees the poet as the giver of life to nature. *Dejection* wishes its *Lady*, Wordsworth, that

> Joy lift her spirit, joy attune her voice;
> To her may all things live, from pole to pole,
> Their life the eddying of her living soul!

Coleridge is wishing Wordsworth the gift of Imagination, to give life to the natural world.

I quote Coleridge's account of the Imagination from the *Biographia Literaria*.

The IMAGINATION then, I consider either as primary, or secondary. The primary IMAGINATION I hold to be the living Power and prime Agent of all human Perception, and as a repetition in the finite mind of the eternal act of creation in the infinite I AM. The secondary Imagination I consider as an echo of the former, co-existing with the conscious will, yet still as identical with the primary in the *kind* of its agency, and differing only in *degree*, and in the *mode* of its operation. It dissolves, diffuses, dissipates, in order to re-create; or where this process is rendered impossible, yet still at all events it struggles to idealize and to unify. It is essentially *vital*, even as all objects (*as* objects) are essentially fixed and dead.

There is no doubt what meaning runs under these words. Coleridge gives several means which the secondary Imagination uses; and all are means to one end, to re-create and make live. 'It is essentially *vital*, even as all objects (*as* objects) are essentially fixed and dead.' The sentence carries a theory which shines with pride in man's life; and which is to shine over the natural world.

But the sentences also make plain that Coleridge wishes to find in this life a kind of ideal, which the secondary Imagination serves. What he writes of the primary Imagination is plainly meant to picture an ideal: 'a repetition in the finite mind of the eternal act of creation in the infinite I AM'. The hint from the bible is to give this something of a religious force. It is a hint that the Imagination in each man stands under a greater Imagination, a Nature which makes all minds. In this meaning the Imagination is an act by which the poet puts himself under an ideal Imagination. Coleridge certainly hankers after this meaning, and others have been willing to take his hankering into the theory. But it has no place in the theory. It is lost whenever Coleridge uses the theory; it is lost as soon as Coleridge turns to the secondary Imagination. For Coleridge's theory is built on one worth alone: the worth of being alive. We cannot think that Coleridge's Imagination is an ideal unless we think that to be alive is an ideal.

We can follow this in Coleridge's own hint from the bible. Coleridge recalls a religious ideal when he takes the Imagination back to the infinite I AM. Coleridge was fond of this quotation from Exodus, 'I am that I am', *Ego sum qui sum*. In the *Biographia Literaria* he tells us what it means to him.

But if we elevate our conception to the absolute self, the great eternal I AM, then the principle of being, and of knowledge, of idea, and of reality; the ground of existence, and the ground of the knowledge of existence, are absolutely identical, Sum quia sum; I am, because I affirm myself to be; I affirm myself to be, because I am.

And he adds the note,

I cannot but express my regret, that in the equivocal use of the word *that*, for *in that*, or *because*, our admirable version has rendered the passage susceptible of a degraded interpretation in the mind of common readers or hearers, as if it were a mere reproof to an impertinent question, I am what I am, which might be equally affirmed of himself by any existent being.

Elsewhere in the *Biographia Literaria* Coleridge tells us that he had been a 'tolerable Hebraist'. No doubt this is his claim to set right the Authorised Version and the Vulgate. Nevertheless Coleridge is wrong and they are right. Scholars are at one in the degraded interpretation: the sentence means 'I am what I am'. It is not my point that Coleridge is wrong. My point is that he should claim so fiercely that he is right. In face of the Authorised Version and the Vulgate, he must read the sentence to mean 'I am because I am'. He cannot see the ideal godhead as set within itself, and not to be understood in other terms: 'I am what I am'. He must justify it by the act of living: 'I am because I am.' To Coleridge, God is the ideal only because he is alive; and he is the ideal of life.

This quarrel of meanings is weighty because Coleridge lays such weight on the words I AM. They are the core of his account of the Imagination, if we are to read an ideal into this account.

The primary IMAGINATION I hold to be the living Power and prime Agent of all human Perception, and as a repetition in the finite mind of the eternal act of creation in the infinite I AM.

Even if we do so, we now find that the ideal I AM is an ideal made of living. It is the giving of all worth to the act of living. Its scale of worth is that which Coleridge put into his praise of the Imagination, that

it is essentially *vital*, even as all objects (*as* objects) are essentially fixed and dead.

This is the worth of Coleridge's Imagination; and I quote again Coleridge's blunt acknowledgment of it.

"How natural!" we say; but the very wonder that furnished the *how* implies that we perceived art at the same moment. We catch the hint from nature itself. Whenever in mountains or cataracts we discover a likeness to anything artificial which we yet know was not artificial, what pleasure!

These sentences also mark the weakness of Coleridge's theory. For if the Imagination does call back to the infinite I AM, the I AM can give life only through living men. That eternal act of creation of which man's Imagination is a repetition in the finite mind can work only by means of finite minds. This can be said against any idealism: the ideals of Sidney and Gosson could work only through man. But Sidney and Gosson granted that in working through man the ideal must be damaged. Their beliefs and their quarrel turned on the study of this damage. Coleridge cannot allow that there is such damage. The act of Imagination of man is the undamaged copy in the finite mind of the ideal Imagination in the infinite I AM.

The secondary Imagination I consider as an echo of the former, co-existing with the conscious will, yet still as identical with the primary in the *kind* of its agency, and differing only in *degree*, and in the *mode* of its operation.

Coleridge may hold with Sidney and Gosson that everything which man makes has only a social worth. But this worth is of the same kind as his ideal worth. To him society itself is the ideal worth; and everything which has social worth therefore partakes in the ideal worth. Everything that shares the life of man is thereby worthy. Nothing is worthy until it shares the life of man.

3

There is another field to which we must follow Coleridge's theory of Imagination. This is the psychological field of the secondary Imagination. Coleridge denies the association theory of Hartley. He believes that the mechanical acts of association do not make up the whole mind. In this belief Coleridge gathers the unmechanical acts of the mind under the name Imagination; he leaves the mechanical acts to the Fancy.

In association then consists the whole mechanism of the reproduction of impressions, in the Aristotelian Psychology. It is the universal law of the *passive* fancy and *mechanical* memory.

That gift of true Imagination, that capability of reducing a multitude into unity of effect, or by strong passion to modify series of thoughts into one predominant thought or feeling.

In this psychological field the theory of Imagination is just that study of

> the affinities of the feelings with words and ideas

of which Coleridge writes to Davy. And in this field 'words and ideas' is a happier phrase than 'natural objects', because the mind does not deal with natural objects. In this field the natural objects are known to the mind only by words and ideas; and only by means of words and ideas can they take order under the living act of the mind.

This is the field into which Coleridge has been followed by such pupils as I. A. Richards. Their own interest in words is endless; and they seek not to set up a root meaning for each word, but to trace the tiny oddities of meaning which may be given to the same word. Their interest matches Coleridge's interest. I have remarked that Wordsworth's Preface to the *Lyrical Ballads* is an essay on poetry, not prosody; and that Coleridge was among the first to mistake it. Coleridge's attack on the Preface is the sign of his interest not in poetry but in the words of poems. I have written of his attack. Here I recall one point of it. Wordsworth has chosen the speech of country men because he holds that

> such men hourly communicate with the best objects from which the best part of language is originally derived.

Coleridge holds against this that the best part of language is not drawn from natural objects, but that

> the best part of human language, properly so called, is derived from reflection on the acts of the mind itself.

The difference between these sentences sums again the difference between two ways of thinking. It does not matter which sentence can be upheld by the more facts. What matters is that Wordsworth sees the poet at last as putting himself under poetry; and Coleridge sees him as mastering poetry.

In Coleridge's thought the tool with which man masters poetry is words. Coleridge attacks the principle by which Wordsworth has chosen his words because it would take this tool from him. For Wordsworth has claimed that words are the symbol of Nature's mastery over man. The poet must put himself under Nature and under poetry by using the speech which the natural world, the symbol of Nature, has given to country men. Against this claim Coleridge must hold at all costs that words are man's own and home-made tool. Therefore Coleridge chooses to attack a lesser point of Wordsworth's Preface. Therefore he claims that man gives his words to himself:

the best part of human language, properly so called, is derived from reflection on the acts of the mind itself.

And therefore he claims that, in any case, the good which Wordsworth finds in the speech of country men may be found in the speech of all men 'of common-sense'.

What principle has Coleridge to put in place of the principle of Wordsworth which he will not allow? Coleridge has forestalled the question.

If it be asked, by what principles the poet is to regulate his own style, if he do not adhere closely to the sort and order of words which he hears in the market, wake, high-road, or plough-field? I reply; by principles, the ignorance or neglect of which would convict him of being no *poet*, but a silly or presumptuous usurper of the name! By the principles of grammar, logic, psychology! In one word by such a knowledge of the facts, material and spiritual, that most appertain to his art, as, if it have been governed and applied by *good sense*, and rendered instinctive by habit, becomes the representative and reward of our past conscious reasonings, insights, and conclusions, and acquires the name of TASTE.

It is disarming of Coleridge to underline *good sense*, no doubt on the principle of blatant camouflage of Edgar Allan Poe's *Purloined Letter*. For, underlined or not, *good sense* must carry the weight of these sentences; and we know as little about Coleridge's *good sense* as about his man of common-sense. Wordsworth tells us clearly how he thinks a poet should write, and why he thinks so. Among a storm of round words, exclamation marks and italics, we learn only this of the principles by which Coleridge would have the poet write: that they follow from a knowledge of the facts about writing poetry, and that they are principles of *good sense*. This is very fine, and it tells us nothing.

Of course Coleridge knows that he is telling us nothing. Of course he is merely ruffling his hair and saying, 'You know what I mean'. The gesture would be endearing if he made it less often: if he did not use *good sense* again and again as a standard of judgment. I. A. Richards has given a chapter to its meaning. He grants that Coleridge scamps it. He does not claim that Coleridge tells us what it means, but that he could tell us if he chose. It is nice to know this. But it leaves us ill at ease with the habit of mind which makes Coleridge tunnel his sentences with bolt-holes down vague phrases.

It is clear what these phrases are to do. Wordsworth and Coleridge built their theories of poetry on the reader's pleasure. Coleridge writes of poetry,

It is the art of communicating whatever we wish to communicate, so as both to express and produce excitement, but for the purpose of immediate pleasure; and each part is fitted to afford as much pleasure, as is compatible with the largest sum in the whole.

The final definition then, so deduced, may be thus worded. A poem is that species of composition, which is opposed to works of science, by proposing for its *immediate* object pleasure, not truth; and from all other species (having *this* object in common with it) it is discriminated by proposing to itself such delight from the *whole*, as is compatible with a distinct gratification from each component *part*.

Wordsworth frankly found this standard too wide, and therefore put hedges round it: the root passions, the natural objects. Coleridge wants to find his hedges within the pleasures themselves. Therefore he weighs pleasure against pleasure, he rules the known pleasure at hand by a vague pleasure in the whole. He is covering his retreat from pleasure; and when the smoke-screen has lifted, the ruling pleasure in the whole has become an artless common-sense, *good sense*, TASTE. All these are private tastes of the reader, which nevertheless are much the same among the readers of one time. Thus they are standards which quietly steal from the reader that judgment by his own pleasure which Wordsworth and Coleridge had claimed to give him.

This theft is striking because Wordsworth and Coleridge had set up the standard of pleasure in order to fight a taste: the taste of the Augustans. Coleridge's *good sense* slinks back to a standard which is oddly like that of the Augustans. Coleridge writes in the Augustan manner,

> GOOD SENSE is the BODY of poetic genius, FANCY its DRAPERY, MOTION its LIFE, and IMAGINATION the SOUL that is everywhere, and in each.

I set beside this a list in another order.

> Design, form, fable, (which is the soul of poetry,)
> Exactness, or consent of parts, (which is the body,)
> Fine metaphors, glittering expressions, and something of a neat cast of verse, (which are properly the dress, gems, or loose ornaments of poetry).

The Fine metaphors of the second list is plainly the same as Coleridge's Fancy; and, in a deeper meaning, the Design of the second list is Coleridge's Imagination. In the second list, Exactness, or consent of parts, is all that sturdy middle work, that body of the poem, which binds together what is apt to the poem. This is Coleridge's *good sense*,

> the facts, material and spiritual, that most appertain to his art, governed and applied by *good sense*.

Much as Coleridge would have disliked the likeness, his *good sense* is thus Pope's consent of parts. For Pope is the writer of the second list. It is entertaining to put beside this Coleridge's words on an

Exactness which Pope upheld. Coleridge writes that when Pope upheld the dramatic unities, he 'was under the common error of his age',

in mistaking for the *essentials* of the Greek stage certain rules, which the wise poets imposed upon themselves, in order....

We need not go on. Coleridge's *good sense* has withered before our eyes, under his own breath. It is the rules and tastes of one time. It makes a false link between the pleasures of a number of readers, because it is merely what a number of readers have been taught to like. It rests upon no inner need of the mind. Coleridge writes that, by its means, the poet's knowledge 'becomes the representative and reward of our past conscious reasonings, insights, and conclusions, and acquires the name of TASTE'. But taste, even in capitals, is not an end which Coleridge has taught us to hold in awe.

Coleridge's pleasure principle has broken down in the wastes of *good sense* and TASTE. The breakdown reaches far. I have studied another theory of Imagination than Coleridge's: the theory of Shelley. I found this theory built on the fake ideal of love, as I find Coleridge's theory built on the fake ideal of life. And I remarked that Shelley ekes out his theory with the principle of pleasure, which makes Coleridge's theory. At the end of the *Defence of Poetry* Shelley tries to find poetry useful by making Use the same as Pleasure. Shelley does not take pleasure so deep as Coleridge. He does not find the weighing of pleasure against pleasure, the ruling of pleasure by pleasure which

Coleridge finds. But the breakdown of Coleridge's pleasure principle is also the breakdown of Shelley. It takes the last prop from the *Defence of Poetry*. Coleridge's theory of Imagination is a richer theory than Shelley's. Coleridge's was a richer and deeper mind than Shelley's. Coleridge was a maker of beginnings in English writing and a discoverer. His theory of Imagination is a discovery. It is a discovery in psychology and in the study of words. It is not a discovery in poetry. Shelley was also a pioneer of psychology and of Imagination; and he passed judgment on Coleridge when he called him 'the subtle-souled psychologist'.

4

I have followed Coleridge's theory of Imagination step by step. Like Wordsworth, and perhaps because Wordsworth has done so, Coleridge sets himself to study man in the face of the natural scene. Like Wordsworth, Coleridge thinks of the poet as deeply moved by the natural scene. But *Dejection* shows that Coleridge's poet draws from nature feelings quite unlike Wordsworth's. Coleridge's poet sees nature as a display for man. The natural scene moves the poet to passion only because he has charged it with passion. Until the poet has charged it the natural scene means nothing to him.

> I may not hope from outward forms to win
> The passion and the life, whose fountains are within.

This belief leads Coleridge to think less of the natural objects than of the words and ideas which stand in the mind for these objects. The natural world is a body of things which is imaged in the mind of each man by a disorderly body of words and ideas. This passive chaos can be used even in this state by man for a pretty and haphazard effect: the effect of Fancy. But the chaos can be given active and living order by the living mind. To Coleridge, order is always a living movement like that of the mind itself,

reducing a multitude into unity of effect, or by strong passion to modify series of thoughts into one predominant thought or feeling.

When the mind gives this lively order to its ideas, and through them to the natural objects, its act is Imagination.

I have therefore read Imagination as that act by which man gives his life to the natural world. And I have shown that Coleridge sees no worth in the natural world but that of recalling the artifice of man. Coleridge grants that the end of Imagination is to be vital. But he claims that in being vital the Imagination is also the image of an ideal creation in the infinite I AM. I have shown that this ideal is at last only the life of man. The infinite I AM itself has worth for Coleridge only because it is alive as man is.

This worship of the life of man can be followed in all that Coleridge writes. I have followed it into his belief that words are the tools of man's mastery of nature. I have followed it into his interest in psychology rather than poetry, even when he studies poems. For example, Coleridge was the first English poet who studied Shakespeare very closely. But he does not study his poetry: he studies his characters. His study shines with flashes of psychological insight. No one has seen deeper into such characters as Macbeth or Hamlet. No one has bettered the brilliant fitful notes in his margins:

> Iago's passionless character, all *will* in intellect.

But this insight also closes, and encloses, his understanding of Shakespeare. In his lectures Coleridge gives some justifications of Shakespeare. Together they run to twenty pages; and begin boldly with a justification of Shakespeare as a poet. But the theme fails Coleridge in three pages; and the rest is a justification of Shakespeare as a maker of characters, on such grounds as these:

> Signal adherence to the great law of nature that opposites tend to attract and temper each other.
>
> Shakespeare's characters are like those in life.
>
> The heterogeneous united as in nature.
>
> The regular high road of human affections.

This is claptrap: Coleridge would surely shudder to see his great law of nature in print. And it is claptrap which springs from an overbearing interest in character. When Coleridge writes of the quarrel scene in *Julius Caesar*, not once but twice,

> I know no part of Shakespeare that more impresses on me the belief of his genius being superhuman than this scene,

he is writing claptrap which is a sad summary of his understanding of Shakespeare.

In *Dejection*, in the theory of Imagination, in the criticism of Wordsworth's Preface, in the Shakespeare criticism, I see Coleridge mastered by his pride in the life of man. The life of man is his only worth; and the only judgment of worth must also come from each man himself. Unlike Wordsworth's, Coleridge's claim that the worth of a poem must be judged by the reader's pleasure is therefore of a piece with his thought. But Coleridge as much as Wordsworth finds that this judgment is too wide to be used. Like Wordsworth, he must hedge it. Unlike Wordsworth, Coleridge tries to find the hedges within man and his pleasures. I have traced the outcome in his shame-faced standards of *good sense* and TASTE. With these, the principle of pleasure as a standard of poetry has failed. For in the Advertisement to the *Lyrical Ballads*, Wordsworth and Coleridge set up the standard of pleasure in order to overthrow a taste which they disliked. When Coleridge comes back to govern pleasure by TASTE he has come to kiss the rod.

Coleridge's pleasure principle is a discovery of psychology. It is not a discovery of poetry. Coleridge sums his belief, his insight and his shortcoming in a single answer.

What is beauty? It is, in the abstract, the unity of the manifold, the coalescence of the diverse; in the concrete, it is the union of the shapely (*formosum*) with the vital.

The sense of beauty is intuitive, and beauty itself is all that inspires pleasure without, and aloof from, and even contrarily to, interest.

This has psychological insight, and it has the short-comings of psychology. And it sums Coleridge's belief: the union of the shapely with the vital. The belief in form and order, the belief in living; and the belief that order is given by the living mind, the Imagination: all are here. Here is the sum of Coleridge's faith that in the living mind of man lies the infinite I AM.

SWINBURNE AND HIS HEIRS

ALGERNON CHARLES SWINBURNE

WORDSWORTH more than any other poet stamped
the speech and the images of the poets after him.
Since he wrote, hardly a poet has been able to choose
his images away from the natural scene. Wordsworth
gave poets a finished tool; and it has since made and
marked the most unlikely poems.

But the thought for which poets have used the
tool has been Coleridge's thought. Coleridge was
strikingly a maker of beginnings. Beginnings of books,
of poems, of thoughts are his work. Two of his best
known poems are unfinished. His best book, the
Biographia Literaria, is a heap of odds and ends, unfinished and only half begun. The poets of the nineteenth century took up these unfinished thoughts.
They took the finished tool from Wordsworth; but
they took their thought, their hope and their unsure-
ness from the lavish beginnings which Coleridge had
left.

The poets after Wordsworth and Coleridge took
over Coleridge's discovery of psychology. They wrote
of psychology in terms of the natural images of
Wordsworth. In part they held to these images
because they were ill at ease with people. They
shirked the work of squaring their notion of people
with what people are. Mary Shelley made this

cruelly clear when she wrote a note to *The Witch of Atlas.*

Shelley shrunk instinctively from portraying human passion, with its mixture of good and evil, of disappointment and disquiet. Such opened again the wounds of his own heart; and he loved to shelter himself rather in the airiest flights of fancy, forgetting love and hate, and regret and lost hope, in such imaginations as borrowed their hues from sunrise or sunset, from the yellow moonshine or paly twilight.

In part these poets held to the natural images of Wordsworth because Coleridge had held to them. Coleridge had already shirked the work for them. I have said that Coleridge thought worthy only that which is alive. So long as this thought was buoyed up by his interest in living men at first hand, it gave strength to his poems. But Coleridge wanted to widen the thought to a principle of living and an infinite I AM. The principle sank to the drugged and dream life of *Christabel* and *Kubla Khan.* These poems are crowded with natural images which have taken on their own bewitched life, the life of the wood in *Christabel*, or *Kubla Khan*'s

> Deep romantic chasm which slanted
> Down the green hill athwart a cedarn cover!
> A savage place! as holy and enchanted
> As e'er beneath a waning moon was haunted
> By woman wailing for her demon-lover!
> And from this chasm, with ceaseless turmoil seething,
> As if this earth in fast thick pants were breathing,
> A mighty fountain momently was forced:
> Amid whose swift half-intermitted burst
> Huge fragments vaulted like rebounding hail.

This nature writhing her wet fronds is the very scene of Shelley: caves, dripping plants, and the weaving of snakes. From it comes the scene of Keats, of Tennyson, and then of Swinburne. All these poets yearned for that which is alive. All shirked the actual life of men 'with its mixture of good and evil, of disappointment and disquiet'. They lacked the hard interest in men, whether Shakespeare's men or the men of Pantisocracy, which had made actual Coleridge's pride in life at his best. They fell into a vague life in a golden age which had been or was to come. They carried on the pappy life of *Christabel* and *Kubla Khan* in which everything is alive and nothing lives. It is as if all the poems of the nineteenth century were written to finish these two unfinished poems.

Swinburne's guide Watts-Dunton has told how poets of his time found in these two poems *The Renascence of Wonder*. The poems linked Coleridge's thought, as the nineteenth century understood it, with Wordsworth's manner as the nineteenth century understood it. I choose Swinburne as the poet in whom I study this thought and manner.

Swinburne's manner has the stamp of Wordsworth. Of course

> O sweet stray sister, O shifting swallow,
>> The heart's division divideth us.
>>> Thy heart is light as a leaf of a tree;
>> But mine goes forth among sea-gulfs hollow
>>> To the place of the slaying of Itylus,
>>>> The feast of Daulis, the Thracian sea

could not have been written by Wordsworth. But that lines on such a theme, with such Miltonic longing

in their names, should hang upon the reader's liking
for birds, trees, and the sea: this is the heirloom of
Wordsworth. It is an heirloom which Swinburne left
to A. E. Housman.

And Swinburne's thought has the stamp of
Coleridge. Swinburne took his awe of the mystery
of living from Coleridge. He took it by way of
Shelley, and he took it a step farther than Shelley.
He took the step into *The Renascence of Wonder*, in
which the poem, the dream, and the life are swaddled
in one mystery. This is an heirloom which Swinburne
left to W. B. Yeats.

Swinburne writes of the poets from whom he
learned,

Coleridge and Keats used nature mainly as a stimulant
or a sedative; Wordsworth as a vegetable fit to shred into
his pot and pare down like the outer leaves of a lettuce
for didactic and culinary purposes. All these doubtless
in their own fashion loved her, for her beauties, for
her uses, for her effects; hardly one for herself.

Turn now to Byron or to Shelley. These two at least
were not content to play with her skirts and paddle in
her shallows. Their passion is perfect, a fierce and blind
desire which exalts and impels their verse into the high
places of emotion and expression. They feed upon nature
with a holy hunger, follow her with a divine lust as of
gods chasing the daughters of men. Wind and fire, the
cadences of thunder and the clamours of the sea, gave
to them no less of sensual pleasure than of spiritual
sustenance. These things they desired as others desire
music or wine or the beauty of women.

The frenzy of these sentences should not make us
forget that they set out to say something. They set

out to say that Shelley and Byron were excited by the images which went into their poems in a way in which Coleridge, Keats, and Wordsworth were not excited by their images. We may doubt whether the list is rightly made; and we may think the excitement bad. But there is no doubt that some poets have had the excitement to which Swinburne points, and that others have not. Why did Swinburne think this excitement good?

We catch a hint of the answer in his sentence,

These two at least were not content to play with her skirts.

Swinburne is thinking of Shelley's own mocking of Wordsworth in *Peter Bell the Third*, that he was

> A kind of moral eunuch,
> He touched the hem of Nature's shift,
> Felt faint—and never dared uplift
> The closest, all-concealing tunic.

This is engaging; but what does it mean? What is it that one should do with nature more than play with her skirts? What is the naked and overwhelming knowledge of nature which Peter Bell shirked? Shelley and Swinburne are at one that it is a sexual knowledge. Swinburne tells us that Shelley followed nature with a divine lust as of gods chasing the daughters of men, and wanted her as others desire music or wine or the beauty of women. This is not like any following of nature which we have met. This is neither imitation of nature, nor holding the mirror up to nature, nor making an other nature. Swinburne's poets must take nature like a lover before he will say that

their passion is perfect, a fierce and blind desire which exalts and impels their verse into the high places of emotion and expression.

Their passion is perfect: the sentence takes us back to a notion of passion which poetry had not held since Gosson taxed it with being 'amarous'.

This sexual and mindless, 'passionate' notion is Swinburne's notion of poetry. It is apt that he should scold Wordsworth and Coleridge for not having it. He writes of Wordsworth,

Meditation and sympathy, not action and passion, were the two main strings of his serene and stormless lyre.

He writes of Coleridge,

The highest lyric work is either passionate or imaginative; of passion Coleridge's has nothing; but for height and perfection of imaginative quality he is the greatest of lyric poets.

For these sentences have a deep irony. Wordsworth and Coleridge were the poets who had urged the readers of the *Lyrical Ballads* that

they should ask themselves if it contains a natural delineation of human passions, human characters, and human incidents; and if the answer be favourable to the author's wishes, that they should consent to be pleased in spite of that most dreadful enemy to our pleasures, our own pre-established codes of decision.

They had overthrown the standards of poetry for the sake of 'human passions, human characters, and human incidents'. They had put pleasure and Wordsworth had put passion at the core of poetry; and now Swinburne their heir finds them passionless.

Certainly Swinburne's passion is not the 'human passions' for which Wordsworth and Coleridge had been ready to give up poetry. Swinburne's passion is a sex-play between the poet and nature, in which not nature but the poet is the god. But Wordsworth and Coleridge had made the beginning for it. Wordsworth had sought the link between nature and the human passions; he had made nature the symbol of the ideal of passion. Sooner or later he was bound to be followed by a poet to whom passion meant lust. Sooner or later this lust would elbow out the passions. The poet who had once felt that

> The sounding cataract
> Haunted me like a passion

would give place to the poet who wanted nature 'as others desire music or wine or the beauty of women'. And the poet of wine, woman and song was bound to find Wordsworth passionless.

Swinburne is looking for life. He is taking Coleridge's principle of living and he is making of it a 'passion' of living. He is trying to make more of living and to make it more real. He taxes Wordsworth that he lacks 'action and passion' because Wordsworth lacks violence and lust. For it seems to Swinburne that violence and lust are the cores of action and passion, and can be touched and are actual. They may be. But Swinburne's use of them as standards in living

is far the more shadowy and abstract. And this is
not chance. Shelley and Swinburne came to these
standards just because the air of the actual in them
is false. These standards allowed the poets to feel
that they were following life 'with a divine lust as of
gods'. But because the standards were so lavish,
Shelley and Swinburne were freed of the need to
touch life as we know it. A nature of

wind and fire, the cadences of thunder and the clamours
of the sea

cannot be asked to stoop to the workaday world. It
can feel that it clamours for life without the need
to think of the living 'human passions, human characters, and human incidents'. It can write

> But life they lay no hand on; life once given
> No force of theirs hath competence to take;
> Life that was given for some divine thing's sake,
> To mix the bitterness of earth with heaven,
> Light with man's night, and music with his breath,
> Dies not, but makes its living food of death.

The words are Swinburne's, and might be Shelley's.
And the thought is Coleridge's, in which life is made
a last principle. When the principle is given its own
life thus, all living things become abstract and lifeless.

The place of life in poetry, of poetry in life were
large questions of the nineteenth century. Peacock
and others asked how poetry helps the everyday life.
Poets from Shelley to Swinburne answered that poetry
is a life-giving principle, and used this vague meaning

of life to shirk Peacock's question. Swinburne had not been writing long when Matthew Arnold tried to make their answer actual, in a sentence which is almost all that is remembered of him,

> Poetry is at bottom a criticism of life.

But Swinburne does not want to make the answer actual. He does not want to think about life in the meaning of Peacock or even of Arnold. Arnold's sentence is not to his liking; and his dislike is worth our study.

Swinburne answers Arnold,

A certain criticism of life, a certain method or scheme of contemplation, a devotion to certain points of view and certain tones of thought, may unquestionably be discerned in the highest work of such poets as Milton, Wordsworth, and Shelley.

But how this fact can possibly be shown to imply that it is this quality which gives them rank as poets; and how the definition of this quality can possibly be strained so as to cover the case of Keats, the most exclusively aesthetic and the most absolutely non-moral of all serious writers on record; these are two questions to which the propounder of such postulates may surely be expected to vouchsafe at least some gleam of a solution.

The points are well made. Swinburne grants that some worthy poets have a singleness of mind and a moral bias which make 'a criticism of life'. But, he claims, it does not follow that their worth therefore lies in this criticism of life. More than this, Swinburne claims that poetic worth cannot lie in the criticism of life, because there are worthy poets who have no singleness of mind and moral bias.

We must allow Swinburne's first claim. Arnold did not prove that poetic worth lies in a criticism of life. He merely pointed to the many poems which have worth which have also a criticism of life. But this claim touches us only by the way. We want to know where Swinburne, not Arnold, found poetic worth. We find a clue in Swinburne's second claim: that there are poems which have worth without having a criticism of life.

Here Swinburne's example is well chosen. Keats did write some worthy poems; and Keats is a poet with little moral thought. True, Arnold tried to find hints of such thoughts in Keats. But he did in effect grant the claim which Swinburne makes here: that Keats and other poets did write worthy poems without singleness of mind and moral bias, in the narrow meaning of these phrases.

Then has Swinburne overthrown Arnold's standard, a criticism of life? Not at all. For Swinburne's claims rest on the meaning which he gives to 'a criticism of life'. Arnold might have allowed that there are worthy poets without singleness of mind and moral bias. But this is not to allow that there are worthy poets without a criticism of life. For only Swinburne has foisted this meaning on a criticism of life.

Swinburne understands this weakness in his claims. He tells Arnold that if the phrase 'a criticism of life' is misunderstood, Arnold has only himself to blame. This is true. But we are not quarrelling about blames but about meanings. Arnold would have done better to make his meaning clear. But Swinburne would have done better to try to understand Arnold's meaning.

What does Swinburne understand Arnold to mean? I quote from another essay.

If, then, precedence among poets is to depend upon their more or less valuable criticism of life, it would seem that Scott's right of precedence over Byron is as unassailable as any critical position can possibly be made.

These examples are not good. Few readers will trouble whether far down the field Scott heads Byron, or Byron heads Scott. And why is Swinburne sure that Scott's criticism of life is better than Byron's? Swinburne gives only one reason, and it is striking: because Scott drew men and women nearer to the life than did Byron.

Set almost any figure drawn by Scott beside almost any figure of Byron's drawing, and the very dullest eye will hardly fail to see the difference between a barber's dummy and a living man fresh from the hand of Velasquez or of God.

And this bears on their criticisms of life by way of another judgment.

Of men, to judge from his writings, Byron knew nothing: of women he knew that it was not difficult to wheedle those who were not unwilling to be wheedled. He also knew that excess of any kind entails a more or less violent and a more or less permanent reaction: and here his philosophy of life subsided into tittering or snivelling silence.

We are not told what was Scott's philosophy of life; but we are told that

On all these points Scott is as far ahead of him as Shakespeare is ahead of Scott.

It is not my place to defend Arnold. But plainly Swinburne is making a caricature of Arnold. Arnold wrote of poetry as a criticism of life. He saw in poetry 'the powerful and beautiful application of ideas to life', and the speech in which man 'comes nearest to being able to utter the truth'. Swinburne tells us that Scott drew lifelike men and women; that Byron knew a few low truisms about men and women; and that these made a philosophy of life. We have seen Swinburne shirking Arnold's meaning once. We have seen him read the criticism of life as singleness of mind and moral bias. Now we see him debase it to a 'philosophy of life' which is made of public-house saws or a gift for catching a likeness. Swinburne does not understand Arnold because he will not understand him. Arnold's criticism of life may be a social standard for poetry. But it is beyond measure more honest and more useful than Swinburne's false ideal of life. It is beyond measure more just than Swinburne's denial of Arnold,

A school of poetry subordinated to any school of doctrine, subjugated and shaped and utilised by any moral idea to the exclusion of native impulse and spiritual instinct, will produce work fit to live when the noblest specimens of humanity are produced by artificial incubation

For Arnold did not ask that poetry should be subordinated to any school of doctrine. He did not ask that it should exclude native impulse and spiritual instinct. He said soberly of good poetry that it is of itself a criticism of life.

Swinburne's denial ends with a flourish, 'when the noblest specimens of humanity are produced by artificial incubation'. The flourish recalls the contradiction within Swinburne's principle of life. The scorn in the words Artificial Incubation is the scorn of a man to whom the act of living, restless generation and becoming, is the last worth. But this act must be careless, mindless, sexual. It must not bear upon life as we know it. It must do no more than hope for a golden chaos.

> I prophesy, with feet upon a grave,
> Of death cast out and life devouring death
> As flame doth wood and stubble with a breath;
> Of freedom, though all manhood were one slave;
> Of truth, though all the world were liar; of love
> That time nor hate can raze the witness of.

Swinburne can write this in the face of his denial of all poetry 'subordinated to any school of doctrine'. For, like Shelley's, his zeal is so vague, his golden age so aimless that he does not need to take his doctrine seriously. This is the poetry of shamefaced doctrine, and the last debasement of Coleridge's life. It is the poetry of those who are happy with their wishes, and can write cheeky attacks on Mammon without ceasing to be 'pure' poets.

2

Coleridge wrote,

The sense of musical delight, with the power of producing it, is a gift of imagination.

Swinburne writes,

The two primary and essential qualities of poetry are imagination and harmony.

The two remarks point to an interest in musical delight and in harmony which is new to poets.

I do not mean that poets before the nineteenth century did not take pains with the sound of their poems. The Elizabethan and Jacobean song-writers took great pains. Dryden and the Augustans after him thought that no poet could be read unless he had smooth numbers. But their sound was not 'musical delight'. The poets who wrote to music did not try to write like music. The delight of Campion's springing pattern,

> Followe thy faire sunne, vnhappy shadowe,
> Though thou be blacke as night,
> And she made all of light,
> Yet follow thy faire sun, vnhappie shadowe,

is not the sounding and shapeless delight, the rolling pleasure in mere words, of

> In Xanadu did Kubla Khan
> A stately pleasure-dome decree:
> Where Alph, the sacred river, ran
> Through caverns measureless to man
>   Down to a sunless sea.

And the Augustan harmony was an elastic but firmly shaped pattern of verse. Certainly Dryden re-wrote Chaucer and Pope re-wrote Donne because they thought that they could make better sounding poems. But it was their sound as poems which they sought to better: not their sound as music. How little even Dryden could do with musical sound we may read in his ode *Alexander's Feast*.

The nineteenth century changed this. The sound which it came to seek in poems is musical sound. The harmony which Swinburne needs is musical harmony. Swinburne says nicely of Byron that

having himself so bad an ear for metre, he may even have imagined that Pope's verse was musical.

Pope's verse is not musical; for it was written to have metre, not music. Swinburne's sentence shows that the two have come to mean the same thing.

This praise for the music of poems is of a piece with another praise which I have quoted from Swinburne. I have quoted his praise of Shelley and Byron because they loved the natural images in their poems for their own sakes. Both praises belong to the social search for how a poem pleases, not for what it is and what it is worth. 'The object is not to examine what is good in each writer, but what has pleased.' The search begins from Coleridge's discovery of psychology, but it grows in Swinburne's discovery of 'pure' poetry. It is the search to make the most of the manner of poems, in order to make the least of their matter.

We have seen Swinburne at this search in his quarrel with Arnold. The poet whose passion is Life cannot allow Arnold's test 'that the greatness of a poet lies in his powerful and beautiful application of ideas to life'. He cannot allow any test. In an essay in which he praises Wordsworth's poems and attacks Wordsworth's principles, Swinburne writes,

> The test of the highest poetry is that it eludes all tests. Poetry in which there is no element at once perceptible and indefinable by any reader or hearer of any poetic instinct may have every other good quality; it may be as nobly ardent and invigorating as the best of Byron's, or as nobly mournful and contemplative as the best of Southey's: if all its properties can easily or can ever be gauged and named by their admirers, it is not poetry— above all, it is not lyric poetry—of the first water.

Taken so far, this is true. For so far it merely says that the poem is more than its parts. If we know everything of a poem when we are given the list of its properties, 'ardent' and 'mournful', it is a poor poem. The properties must be held together by something which at last is the poem. We can give names to this holding together, Order or Nature or Imagination; but it is different in kind from the properties, it is a holder and maker of properties. And it cannot be judged by mechanical tests because tests judge only properties. So far Swinburne is right,

> If all its properties can easily or can ever be gauged and named by their admirers, it is not poetry—above all, it is not lyric poetry—of the first water.

But Swinburne cannot stop there. He must take one step farther.

There must be something in the mere progress and resonance of the words, some secret in the very motion and cadence of the lines, inexplicable by the most sympathetic acuteness of criticism.

This is a bold *non sequitur*. We are at one that the properties are not enough. We are at one that 'there must be something' more. But why must this something lie 'in the mere progress and resonance of the words'? Why must the poetic core lie in 'the very motion and cadence of the lines' and nowhere else?

The answer which Swinburne has in mind is: Because the properties make up the matter of the poem, and therefore the something must lie outside the matter, that is in the manner. This answer will not bear looking at. For if there is such a thing at all as the matter of a poem, away from the manner, it is certainly more than the sum of the properties. The matter is that supposed re-telling of the poem towards which each fuller and fuller re-telling moves step by step. This supposed re-telling may be too unwieldy to make; and no reader may know enough to make it. But in theory there is no reason why at last it should not say everything in and round the poem. It cannot re-tell some delights of the poem: quips, tricks of speech and sound, hints of other poems. These must therefore be taken to belong to the manner. But when we have picked from the re-telling all the properties, the ardent and the mournful, we shall not have taken everything from it. We shall have left the linking of just these properties in just this way, which makes the poem a thing alone. The something of the poem may then lie in this linking. Certainly there is then a place for it elsewhere than in the mere progress and resonance of the words.

I allow myself to make this point again: because Swinburne's mistake is made again and again to-day, whether by psychological critics like I. A. Richards, or by 'pure' critics like A. E. Housman. Swinburne counts off the 'properties' of a poem, and finds that they do not give the worth of the poem. The worth must therefore lie in what is left; and Swinburne sees nothing left but 'the mere progress and resonance of the words'. But let us begin at the other end. Let us take any poem whose progress and resonance is not in doubt: almost any nineteenth century poem, Blake's *Milton*, *Kubla Khan*, *In Memoriam*, the *Atalanta* choruses, the *Echo* poems of Hopkins. I do not mean mere pieces of mouthing, but poems whose sound gives us an uncommon pleasure, and which we go on hearing in the ear after the mind thinks of something else. Nevertheless we all know better poems than these, whose sound is less pleasing. It follows that the worth of poems cannot lie in the sound. We are tempted to say that it follows that the worth must lie in the matter. But this is such a *non sequitur* as I have damned in Swinburne. What follows is that a poem has worth only because it has matter as well as manner. The worth may be a play between matter and manner. It may be a play in the matter which can take place only by virtue of the manner. It is certainly not 'in the mere progress and resonance of the words'.

Of course sound is a need in poems. A poem cannot get on without certain kinds of sound, any more than it can get on without paper and printer's ink. But it does not follow that the sound, the paper and ink, is a worth in the poem. These things are merely needed in order that the poem shall be able to have worth at all. If what is needed and what is worthy are sometimes the same things, this is by chance. Nothing is likely to please us and to move us as poetry does unless it has a certain progress and resonance of the words. And nothing is likely to reach to that soul in us where we judge worth unless it has pleased us and moved us. To have a certain kind of sound, thereby to please and to move, are therefore needs without which no poem can have worth. But they do not therefore make any part of the worth. And this is as true of the matter of poems. All that we can learn from such reasoning is that without both manner and matter there is no poem. And this does not help us to find the worth of poems.

Swinburne tries to find the worth in the manner of poems, and at the cost of their matter. He praises Shelley and Byron because they loved the images in their poems for themselves. He seeks 'something in the mere progress and resonance of the words, some secret in the very motion and cadence of the lines'. All this is a 'passion' for the materials of poems whose end is to shirk the matter. We all know this end in

Swinburne's poems: their frenzy of images and sound
round the vague life of a golden age.

> Ye forces without form and viewless powers
> That have the key of all our years in hold,
> That prophesy too late with tongues of gold,
>   In a strange speech whose words are perished hours,
> I witness to you what good things ye give
> As ye to me what evil while I live.

I do not write of these poems here. Swinburne is not
a poet without thought. He has some of that criticism
of life which he attacks so fiercely. He has Shelley's
themes, hatred of tyranny, a challenging of death,
a living in the golden age, sorrow at the classical
sorrows. But his life in the senses masters these
thoughts. Swinburne makes Saint Dorothy say that
death

> Hath soft flower of tender-coloured hair
> Grown on his head, and a red mouth as fair
> As may be kissed with lips.

It is the picture of his poems; and the end of the
search for image and sound is this soft and sexual
verse. I am more interested in the search than in the
verse.

But there are two strands which run from his verse
which I follow. Read

> Lo, this is she that was the world's delight;
>   The old grey years were parcels of her might;
> The strewings of the ways wherein she trod
>   Were the twain seasons of the day and night.

This was not written by W. B. Yeats; it was written
by Swinburne. And read

> We are not sure of sorrow,
>   And joy was never sure;
> To-day will die to-morrow;
>   Time stoops to no man's lure.

This was not written by A. E. Housman; it was also written by Swinburne. The two passages show how far the strands of Swinburne's manner reach. They reach to Yeats and Housman. Yeats and Housman did not copy Swinburne: Swinburne had merely written already what they were about to write. For Swinburne is the sum of nineteenth century poetry.

The strands which I have unravelled in him are the strands of this poetry. They go back to the discoveries of Wordsworth and Coleridge; and they go by way of Coleridge. Wordsworth stamped them with the images of nature; but the nature is Coleridge's nature of stage displays and a bewitched life. Swinburne has Coleridge's faith in life; and has made it lifeless, because he has cut it off from Coleridge's interest in men. I have shown how hard Swinburne holds away from the common life which Arnold tried to touch. The life which Swinburne seeks is as unreal as the nature which he has from Coleridge. Like Shelley, he wants to be in revolt against his time without changing his time. And Swinburne's criticism is indeed full of the moral tone of his time. Like Shelley, Swinburne is a poet of shamefaced doctrine.

The type of Swinburne's vague life is the images of his own poems. And Swinburne seeks the same vague life in the images and sounds of poems. The images must live for themselves, the sounds must please by their own music. Nothing must be part of a thinking poem, everything must have its own mindless and sexual life. Swinburne finds the worth of poems in images and above all in sound. I have shown on what flimsy reasoning such worth rests. Yet this worth is on the tongue of every critic since Swinburne: good critics to-day point to the sound with his awe. For we must not mistake Swinburne. He was not a bad critic. Like Arnold, he was a better pleader for poetry than critic of it. But he always upheld the good, he seldom upheld the bad. When he did uphold the bad it was because he shared the faith which had made the bad. He upheld Shelley, because he was Shelley's heir. But he did not misjudge Shelley. At a time when Shelley's *Defence of Poetry* was about to become a school primer he wrote,

The value of Shelley's prose writings is almost purely subjective; they would have no interest whatever for any imaginable reader if they threw no light on the character which helped to shape and to colour, to modify and to quicken, the genius of a poet.

Few critics of Shelley have been so outspoken. And the criticism gives us the hint how we must read Swinburne. We must read him not for himself but for something else. We must read him because he is the sum of the nineteenth century. And the nineteenth century still writes our criticism.

ALFRED EDWARD HOUSMAN

I

SWINBURNE believed that the worth of poems lies in their manner. His belief in 'pure' poetry has been well put to-day by A. E. Housman. It is worth our while to study it as Housman puts it in his one essay, *The Name and Nature of Poetry*.

We shall best understand how Housman is putting it if we begin with a sentence from the middle of his essay.

> When I hear anyone say, with defiant emphasis, that Pope was a poet, I suspect him of calling in ambiguity of language to promote confusion of thought.

This clears the air. We know what we are not talking about. We are not talking about poetry in the meaning in which the *Oxford Book of English Verse* is a book of poetry. We are talking only about some poems chosen for some one grace; and we are putting aside all the poems which have long been judged to be good which are without this grace. So Housman puts aside the poems of the Metaphysicals and of the Augustans. They are not poetry. Then what is poetry?

> 'But no man may deliver his brother, nor make agreement unto God for him', that is to me poetry so moving that I can hardly keep my voice steady in reading it. And that this is the effect of language I can ascertain by experiment: the same thought in the bible version,

'None of them can by any means redeem his brother, nor give to God a ransom for him', I can read without emotion.

Poetry is not the thing said but a way of saying it.

The sentences carry the belief of Swinburne: 'something in the mere progress and resonance of the words, some secret in the very motion and cadence of the lines'. But they give it a new air. The judgment which leads Housman to Swinburne's belief is a judgment from the feelings and from the body, 'I can hardly keep my voice steady'. Housman blurs the question whether these feelings are indeed made by the way of saying it, or whether they are merely made unbearable by the way of saying it. Like Swinburne, he finds the worth in the way of saying it: but he judges the way by his feelings. Thus he seems to set up a standard more actual than Swinburne's. Housman even writes,

There is a conception of poetry which is not fulfilled by pure language and liquid versification, with the simple and so to speak colourless pleasure which they afford, but involves the presence in them of something which moves and touches in a special and recognisable way.

And I think that to transfuse emotion—not to transmit thought but to set up in the reader's sense a vibration corresponding to what was felt by the writer—is the peculiar function of poetry.

This has the air of going beyond Swinburne's belief. The air is false. Swinburne was no more content than Housman with pure language and liquid versification, if these mean something which gives only a colourless pleasure. Housman's further belief that to transfuse emotion is the peculiar function of poetry is merely the claim for the colour which Swinburne would have asked from the mere progress and resonance of the words. Housman and Swinburne are at one that the colour must have no thought in it.

Housman's feelings are bodily feelings: 'Poetry indeed seems to me more physical than intellectual'. They grow from the bodily life of the senses. Have such feelings a place in the judgment of poetry? Housman quotes the *Book of Common Prayer*, and says,

That is to me poetry so moving that I can hardly keep my voice steady in reading it.

Very well. But there are sentences which shake the voices of other readers: sentences from love letters, the news of a friend's death, the number of men who were blinded in the War. Does their unsteadiness make these sentences poetry? Or would it make them poetry only if it were caused by the way of saying it? Housman is not clear. He holds that a poem should move the feelings. He holds that the feeling gives the poem worth, and that the feeling at last is the poem. But he holds that the poem and therefore the feeling is not the thing said but a way of saying it. Since this is not true of every feeling, we learn suddenly that Housman is not speaking of the feelings as one. He is speaking only of some feelings: those which are ruled by words, those which shake the voice. We now understand his dislike of the Metaphysicals and of the Augustans. He does not dislike them for their lack of feeling. He dislikes them for their lack of one feeling, the sadness and longing which shake the voice. When he blames Pope he writes,

> But not even in the Elegy to the memory of an unfortunate lady does the fire burn clear of smoke, and truth of emotion do itself full justice in naturalness and purity of diction.

But why choose the *Elegy to the Memory of an Unfortunate Lady*? Why not choose *Windsor Forest*? Because Housman is only looking for elegies and sadness. He is looking not for 'truth of emotion' but for that emotion which shakes the voice. He is even ready to go to bodily ill-health in order to call out this emotion.

> I have seldom written poetry unless I was rather out of health, and the experience, though pleasurable, was generally agitating and exhausting.

When Edgar Allan Poe tells how he planned *The Raven*, he writes,

> Regarding, then, Beauty as my province, my next question referred to the *tone* of its highest manifestation— and all experience has shown that this tone is one of *sadness*. Beauty of whatever kind, in its supreme development, invariably excites the sensitive soul to tears. Melancholy is thus the most legitimate of all the poetical tones.

Housman goes a step farther. To him sadness *is* poetry, and the only poetry.

I study some sentences which search for this sadness.

In these six simple words of Milton—

> Nymphs and shepherds, dance no more—

what is it that can draw tears, as I know it can, to the eyes of more readers than one? What in the world is there to cry about? Why have the mere words the physical effect of pathos when the sense of the passage is blithe and gay? I can only say, because they are poetry, and find their way to something in man which is obscure and latent, something older than the present organisation of his nature, like the patches of fen which still linger here and there in the drained lands of Cambridgeshire.

Poetry indeed seems to me more physical than intellectual.

Experience has taught me, when I am shaving of a morning, to keep watch over my thoughts, because, if a line of poetry strays into my memory, my skin bristles so that the razor ceases to act. This particular symptom is accompanied by a shiver down the spine; there is another which consists in a constriction of the throat and a precipitation of water to the eyes.

I stop here, because the words 'a precipitation of water to the eyes' sum the false seriousness and the manliness-ill-at-ease of Housman's essay. They warn us that Housman is speaking in a mood at once sprightly and shamefaced, in which he will shirk his meaning. And they throw a cruel light on his test, 'not the thing said but a way of saying it'. Housman's way of saying tears is 'a precipitation of water to the eyes'.

Housman has quoted the third song from *Arcades*.

> Nymphs and Shepherds dance no more
>   By sandy *Ladons* Lillied banks.
> On old *Lycæus* or *Cyllene* hoar,
>   Trip no more in twilight ranks,
> Though *Erymanth* your loss deplore,
>   A better soyl shall give ye thanks.
> From the stony *Mænalus*,
> Bring your Flocks, and live with us,

> Here ye shall have greater grace,
> To serve the Lady of this place.
> Though *Syrinx* your *Pans* Mistres were,
> Yet *Syrinx* well might wait on her.
> Such a rural Queen
> All *Arcadia* hath not seen.

We may doubt whether this lovely song goes far enough beyond pure language and liquid versification to be called either gay or sad. But grant that the meaning is gay. Do the first six words move us to tears? Housman says that they move 'more readers than one' to tears; but we may still believe that they move few of us to tears. Now to the question, What is it that can draw tears? there are always two answers: the sadness of the words, or the tearfulness of the reader. The second answer is not ruled out because more than one reader has cried. Housman says in this essay that few who like poems like the poetry in them. He can therefore claim that those who do not cry at these words are those who like something else than the poetry. But this still leaves us, in order to find the poetry, to look among those who do cry for what makes them cry. What reader will cry, and what will he cry over?

The reader who will cry will certainly be a learned reader. If he reads beyond the six words he will meet names which carry all the Miltonic longing, to the learned reader. If he reads only the six words he must feel deeply the memories which lie in the words Nymphs and Shepherds. These memories are not clear thoughts; they are not part of the blithe

and gay meaning. They call back to the Arcadias
of all poets. They recall the loss of all Arcadias, and
the mourning of all poets for their loss. They recall
the lost Nymphs and the dead Shepherds, and the
poets who mourned Arcadia when they mourned for
their loss. In England, Spenser, Shakespeare, Jonson,
Milton himself, Dryden, and a score of others wrote
poems which mourn the dead Shepherd. They were
mourning for the golden age and for those who were
young and handsome. We need not wonder that
Housman found the memory sad. And the words
Nymphs and Shepherds do more. They call to a later
history, of Arcadian make-believe, the picnics in
Arden, the fancy dress of Marie Antoinette in her
dairy. We know that this lavender folly is gone. We
know that the dairy maids played on the brink of
death. We know that the play is done, and that the
squalor which they played to hide is not done.
'Nymphs and Shepherds dance no more' is so frighten-
ingly apt to this knowledge that the reader may be
forgiven if horror masters the meaning for a moment.
And all this is a matter for tears; and shows that when
Milton wrote, he foreshadowed feelings and memories
so great that we must stare. But it does not make the
poem. Neither is the poem made by the lovely fall of
the words. 'Dance no more' closes a line as the young
Milton could close it, with an ending like falling
asleep. The fall is apt to the memories and is needed
to wake them. And the reader needs the memories if
he is to take pleasure in the poem. But if he finds the
worth of the poem in them he is a bad reader. For

words like Nymphs, Shepherds, Syrinx, Arcadia are symbols for a historical change, and so for our bookish feeling for the past. This feeling has a place in the pleasure which we take in the poem. But if we allow it to master the poem, we give to the symbols a feeling which is too great for the matter. Such feeling is hysteria. The maudlin and bookish longing which draws from these symbols a precipitation of water to the eyes is hysteria.

There are good poems which carry the sadness which is Housman's Poetry. There are more bad poems which carry it. And there are good poems which do not carry it. The *Ancient Mariner*, the *Intimations of Immortality* are poems which carry beyond measure more tragedy than anything which Housman quotes. They carry none of his petty sadness. We see that Housman has not cut down the list of what he will call poems sharply enough. It is not enough to cut out the Metaphysical and the Augustan poets. There are greater poets who fail his test of sadness. Housman's true poet must be chosen very carefully.

For me the most poetical of all poets is Blake. I find his lyrical note as beautiful as Shakespeare's and more beautiful than anyone else's; and I call him more poetical than Shakespeare, even though Shakespeare has so much more poetry, because poetry in him preponderates more than in Shakespeare over everything else, and instead of being confounded in a great river can be drunk pure from a slender channel of its own. Shakespeare is rich in thought, and his meaning has power of itself to move us, even if the poetry were not there: Blake's meaning is often unimportant or virtually non-existent, so that we can listen with all our hearing to his celestial tune.

It is hard to be sure what these sentences mean. But they must mean one of two things. Either Blake is the best poet, or he is not the best poet. Let us take it first that he is not the best poet. Certainly Housman seems to imply that there are better poets and that Shakespeare is a better poet. But Housman calls Blake the most poetical of all poets. The worth of the better poets must therefore lie in something else than their poetry. Is Housman granting that even he listens for something else than poetry?

I am convinced that most readers, when they think that they are admiring poetry, are deceived by inability to analyse their sensations, and that they are really admiring, not the poetry of the passage before them, but something else in it, which they like better than poetry.

It seems that most readers are right. Housman's Poetry is not worth, and only Housman need like it better than worth. Housman is granting that his wilful use of the word Poetry for something which brings a precipitation of water to the eyes is a false use.

There is only one way out of this. We must take the sentences to mean that Blake is the best poet. We must deny that Shakespeare and others are better poets. They may call up other awes, but Blake is the best poet. Perhaps Housman did mean this behind the blurring of 'the most poetical of poets'. If he did, the sentences are the *reductio ad absurdum* of his meaning. Blake is a good poet. But if we define poetry so that we prove him the best poet, we prove something which is absurd; and we must go back to change our definition. Housman said that 'all my life long the best literature of several languages has been my favourite recreation'. He knew the *Iliad*, the choruses of Aeschylus and Sophocles, the plays of Shakespeare and Racine, the poems of Dante, Milton and Goethe. With this knowledge, he claimed that Blake is the most poetical of all poets. Whatever he meant, his meaning of Poetry stands foolishly to be mocked by itself.

I do not grudge Housman his pleasure in sad sound. What I grudge is that he who liked poems only for their ache and longing should pertly tell others that

they are really admiring, not the poetry of the passage before them, but something else in it, which they like better than poetry.

What I grudge is that he who belittled poetry to mean only sad sound should brazenly tell others to 'beware of treating the word poetry as chemists have treated the word salt'.

If we apply the word poetry to an object which does not resemble, either in form or content, anything which has heretofore been so called, not only are we maltreating and corrupting language, but we may be guilty of disrespect and blasphemy.

For it is Housman's 'object', which makes Blake the most poetical of all poets, which does not resemble poetry.

Housman's theory fences off a small plot of feeling and calls it Poetry. This is more than a theory: it is a cast of mind. I shall study this cast in Housman's

poems. I have studied something of it in Swinburne.
Swinburne and Housman seem more unlike than
like. Swinburne's abandon, his writing in the senses,
his talkativeness, his careless and headlong air, and
his lack of sad longing are unlike Housman's manner.
But under the manners lies a deeper likeness. Both
ask the same things of poetry, that it should move
them by its sounds, and that it should move them in
the senses. Both stand against any theory which
seeks to make actual that very longing for life which
fills their poems with dreams. For both have the
longing of scholars for the past, its books and its
names. Both seek a 'pure' poetry which shall not
think.

2

The matter of Housman's poems is simple. It holds
to a few feelings: the feelings of love, of friendship,
of honour, of bravery; and the feeling that we must
look at these bravely and know that they are pointless.
These feelings are not praised and they are not
debated. It is taken for granted that they are in all
men. And it is not debated that they are at odds
with themselves. We see that they are at odds. If
love, friendship, honour, bravery are worthy feelings
which give point to living, why does Housman write

> Lie down, lie down, young yeoman;
>   What use to rise and rise?
> Rise man a thousand mornings
>   Yet down at last he lies,
>   And then the man is wise.

If they are pointless feelings and death is their pointless end, why does he write

> If it chance your eye offend you,
>   Pluck it out, lad, and be sound:
> 'Twill hurt, but here are salves to friend you,
>   And many a balsam grows on ground.
>
> And if your hand or foot offend you,
>   Cut it off, lad, and be whole;
> But play the man, stand up and end you,
>   When your sickness is your soul.

The brunt of these two sets of feelings makes the
sadness of Housman's poems. This is the sadness which
Housman calls Poetry. And it is the point of his
sadness that it shall be at odds within itself. It shall
grow from holding two feelings at once which no force
can hold together. When Housman chooses to hold at
once the feeling for love, friendship, honour, bravery,
and the feeling that these feelings are pointless, he
makes sure that he shall fail. It is a foreseen defeat
and a planned sadness.

Housman measures each feeling against death. If
he does wish to live it is not for these feelings but for
a pleasure of the senses: the spring country, some
tipsiness. He has summed these wishes.

> Could man be drunk for ever
>   With liquor, love, or fights,
> Lief should I rouse at morning
>   And lief lie down of nights.
>
> But men at whiles are sober
>   And think by fits and starts,
> And if they think, they fasten
>   Their hands upon their hearts.

The thinking mood is a mood of death, from which-
ever of Housman's two sets of feelings it grows. And
we learn that indeed the mood does not grow from
the feelings, but that the feelings grow from Housman's dwelling on death. We learn that one set of
feelings is that with which he is willing to face death;
and these feelings then seem to him worthy,

> So here are things to think on
>   That ought to make me brave,
> As I strap on for fighting
>   My sword that will not save.

The other feelings fear death, which then seems to
him to dwarf every feeling,

> Lovers lying two and two
>   Ask not whom they sleep beside,
> And the bridegroom all night through
>   Never turns him to the bride.

Thus the steady place of death in Housman's poems
is neither chance nor foible. It is the making of the
poems.

We therefore learn to see deeply into Housman's
sadness. He is sad because he writes in an aimless
welter of standards which he cannot hold together.
Not only two standards are at odds. Every standard
is called on, now in this poem, now in that. Every
poem is at odds with every other. For every poem has
a standard and makes a judgment of living: but
Housman has no standard. Housman can judge the
acts of life with one sentence only: that we must die.
But death is not a standard for life. It may be, as

Housman thought, that man is helpless and worthless. But man is not worthless because he is helpless. He is not helpless and worthless because he must die. Man must still get on with living.

> The troubles of our proud and angry dust
> Are from eternity, and shall not fail.
> Bear them we can, and if we can we must.

And he must live as well, by standards as fixed, whether his pains will seem pointless in death or not. He must make choices which death makes neither easier nor smaller. Housman says this himself.

> But from my grave across my brow
> Plays no wind of healing now,
> And fire and ice within me fight
> Beneath the suffocating night.

In face of this Housman writes as if death judges and dwarfs life. Therefore his poems allow reader and writer to flood themselves with sadness while they shirk choices and standards.

Housman's poems reel from one standard to another. If one poem finds love worthy,

> Ah, past the plunge of plummet,
> In seas I cannot sound,
> My heart and soul and senses,
> World without end, are drowned,

the poem over the page will find it pointless,

> The nettle nods, the wind blows over,
> The man, he does not move,
> The lover of the grave, the lover
> That hanged himself for love.

If one poem is glad that a young man has left life before honour, the next will say that silly lads always want to leave their life. And whatever the standard, Housman feels that he himself who is without a standard is smaller by it. The lads who have gone off to play, to war, and to be hanged are always better lads than Housman.

> My dreams are of a field afar
>   And blood and smoke and shot.
> There in their graves my comrades are,
>   In my grave I am not.

> I too was taught the trade of man
>   And spelt the lesson plain;
> But they, when I forgot and ran,
>   Remembered and remain.

But Housman has not forgotten the lesson. He has merely learnt another lesson from other friends. Other friends see the trade of man otherwise.

> But since the man that runs away
> Lives to die another day,
> And cowards' funerals, when they come,
> Are not wept so well at home,

> Therefore, though the best is bad,
> Stand and do the best, my lad;
> Stand and fight and see your slain,
> And take the bullet in your brain.

This is more bitter than to call himself coward: Housman is belittling his feelings more. And this is Housman's most tender sadness: to belittle the very feeling which makes the poem. It gives irony to the sadness, it makes it rueful as well as wistful.

Housman is ashamed of the tear which he drops, and yet he must show the tear and show the shame. This is the shamefaced manliness of 'a precipitation of water to the eyes'. This is the swooning pain of

> Lovers lying two and two
>   Ask not whom they sleep beside,
> And the bridegroom all night through
>   Never turns him to the bride.

Housman is sad that a passion held high in life is thrown down by death. But the verse has a second range of sadness. Housman has chosen love as the falling passion, and he has underlined it with tender words like bridegroom, in order to heighten the falling passion. But it is not heightened in order that its fall may seem greater. There is no stress on the fall, only on the level pointlessness of the result. Then why is the falling passion heightened? It is to mark the littleness of the poem itself, set by the side of the passion: set by the side of love and of death. Housman is asking the reader's pity not for the dead but for himself and his poem. And the reader is not to pity his suffering but the silly thought and feeling which he draws from his suffering.

> The pools and rivers wash so clean
>   The trees and clouds and air,
> The like on earth was never seen,
>   And oh that I were there.

> These are the thoughts I often think
>   As I stand gazing down
> In act upon the cressy brink
>   To strip and dive and drown;

But in the golden-sanded brooks
  And azure meres I spy
A silly lad that longs and looks
  And wishes he were I.

Here Housman belittles the longing to die which
makes his poems. He finds it as silly as the longing
of the lad from the other world to live. This is
Housman's most subtle tool of sadness: to make the
reader pity him for a weakness which the reader is
also asked to despise, and which Housman despises.
I quote a poem from *A Shropshire Lad* which uses the
tool most skilfully.

'Is my team ploughing,
  That I was used to drive
And hear the harness jingle
  When I was man alive?'

Ay, the horses trample,
  The harness jingles now;
No change though you lie under
  The land you used to plough.

'Is football playing
  Along the river shore,
With lads to chase the leather
  Now I stand up no more?'

Ay, the ball is flying,
  The lads play heart and soul;
The goal stands up, the keeper
  Stands up to keep the goal.

'Is my girl happy,
  That I thought hard to leave,
And has she tired of weeping
  As she lies down at eve?'

> Ay, she lies down lightly,
>   She lies not down to weep:
> Your girl is well contented.
>   Be still, my lad, and sleep.
>
> 'Is my friend hearty,
>   Now I am thin and pine,
> And has he found to sleep in
>   A better bed than mine?'
>
> Yes, lad, I lie easy,
>   I lie as lads would choose;
> I cheer a dead man's sweetheart,
>   Never ask me whose.

Housman leads us step by step here. The first answer tells the dead man that he is not missed. The second answer perhaps hints already that Housman has stepped into his shoes. For it may mean that the dead man was the village goalkeeper; and earlier in *A Shropshire Lad* Housman has told us that he is the goalkeeper now. The third answer suddenly shows that Housman is ashamed of something. He suddenly tries to stop the dead man's questions: 'Be still, my lad, and sleep'. And the fourth answer shows us what it is. Housman has taken the dead man's sweetheart. But the reader is no longer asked to pity the dead man for his loss: he is asked to pity Housman. The reader is asked to think that Housman is a cad for taking the sweetheart; and he is also asked to pity him and to be sad with him that this is the way of life. He is asked to share Housman's haphazard of standards. Here is Housman's feeling of honour, that it is caddish to take the dead man's sweetheart. Here is Housman's feeling that honour is pointless, which made him take the sweetheart. And here is his search to make honour and dishonour one, in the soft irony of 'I lie as lads would choose'. They make a sadness which tangles together the littleness of the writer, of the reader who pities him, and of the poem which moves to pity. Housman has taken the last step of self-belittling. He is asking the reader to pity him for being such a pitiable fellow. He is saying 'Not only is this a sad and silly poem; there is the untold sadness that we should be moved by it'.

This is the sadness in which Housman finds Poetry. These are the feelings and these are the poems which *The Name and Nature of Poetry* is written to defend. The poems damn themselves. They have no standards. They despise their own feelings. They move the reader only by their own self-belittling. They judge them-selves, and find themselves little. They leave Housman only two defences, which he took in *The Name and Nature of Poetry*. One defence is that sadness and longing make a worthy poem however they are got. This makes Housman plead for tearfulness in a blithe and gay poem of Milton. This makes him boast that 'I have seldom written poetry unless I was rather out of health'. He is claiming that maudlin feelings are poetry, whether we get them from Milton, from ill-health, or from the self-pity and belittling of his own poems. The other defence is that 'poetry is not the thing said but a way of saying it'. This lingers on Blake's celestial tune and on the workmanship of Housman's own poems. Housman's poems have little right to this defence. They are short poems, but they

are not the spare poems which Housman set himself
to write. They are as wordy and as clumsy as the
poems of Swinburne, because the ratio of words to
thought in them is as high. But I need not meet this
defence. I have shown in Housman's own judgment
of Blake that he cannot uphold this belief in 'pure'
poetry.

'Pure' poetry, in Swinburne, in Housman, is no
poetry. Its beauty of sound is overshadowed by the
worth of the best poems. It can be eked out only by
its echo in the feelings. But they must be feelings
cut off from thought and from life: the pure 'passions'
for nature which Swinburne praises, the narrow sadness and longing which is Housman's poetry. I have
shown that we cannot respect Swinburne's passions.
And I have shown that Housman himself did not
respect his own feelings.

WILLIAM BUTLER YEATS

I

DURING forty years W. B. Yeats has changed the manner of his poems strikingly. He made his fame with a soft and frenzied verse. He has kept it with a harsh and thoughtful, almost a didactic verse. But Yeats has hardly changed the matter of his poems at all. Almost every poem he has written debates the same theme: the poet's place in the world. Far more pointedly than his criticism, Yeats's poems debate a theory of poetry; and I study his theory in them.

Yeats debates his theme less in words than in images. This is the other steady mark of his poems: that whatever their manner, they are heavy with images. Once the images were to make a stiff pattern on the surface of the poem. Now they make the thought within the poem. It is less a thought than a brooding, which in the end is summed in the images of the poem. Yeats now believes that the image gathers the hidden knowledge of man like a lens, and throws it out again in a halo of light. 'No mind is more valuable than the images it contains.' And he believes that the pleasure which the image gives can itself make a thought and even an ideal. Sidney and other poets thought that man's pleasures and his ideal are at odds; but Yeats has shut up this battle within the image.

In his early poems Yeats does hold an ideal. His

ideal is purpose; he believes that what is purposeful is thereby worthy. He does not praise one kind of purpose: Christian purpose, or the purpose which drives lovers, or the purpose which drives to war. His ideal is purpose in itself, and every kind of purpose. For purpose gives order to our aimless living and lifts it above living. Therefore it gives worth to living. Yeats sees his own poems as worthy because they have a purpose: to praise the purposeful. And he sees the deeds of others as worthy because they are driven by a purpose.

We may read this very clearly in *The Countess Cathleen*. The Countess Cathleen hears that her starving people are selling their souls for bread. In order to save them she sells her own soul and feeds them with the price. Nevertheless her soul does not go to hell. Her deed has been purposeful, and therefore it wins grace. It lifts her bartered soul to heaven. The greatness of the Countess Cathleen's deed is not measured vaguely by its self-sacrifice. It is measured exactly by its purpose. We may think that in *The Countess Cathleen* the deed is measured by one kind of purpose: Christian purpose. Yeats has said that Blake believed

that the sympathy with all living things, sinful and righteous alike, which the imaginative arts awaken, is that forgiveness of sins commanded by Christ.

We may think that the Countess Cathleen's deed springs from this sympathy: like the Christian forgiveness of Shelley's Prometheus, and the Christian blessing of Coleridge's Ancient Mariner. But it is not the sympathy alone which wins grace for the Countess Cathleen. It is not enough for her to forgive her people like Prometheus, or to bless them unaware like the Ancient Mariner. She plans to save the people whom she loves as purposefully as the 'imaginative arts' are planned; and it is the planned and active, the purposeful deed which wins grace for her. Her grace *is* purpose.

Yeats's belief here is also his belief in the worth of the imaginative arts. He finds them worthy because they are purposeful; that is, from the same cause which makes the great deeds of living worthy. Yeats's belief at this time couples poetry with great living as Sidney coupled them. Yeats's purpose is an ideal of poetry like Sidney's Virtue, which can sometimes throw its light over living. The Countess Cathleen, like Stella, is the symbol of Virtue.

For Yeats wants to find its symbol in a woman. True, women seem to be purposeless creatures; and their beauty seems to put the purposed beauties of the poet to shame.

> O cloud-pale eyelids, dream-dimmed eyes,
> The poets labouring all their days
> To build a perfect beauty in rhyme
> Are overthrown by a woman's gaze
> And by the unlabouring brood of the skies.

But this is only a seeming contradiction; for when Yeats makes a like complaint again,

> A line will take us hours maybe;
> Yet if it does not seem a moment's thought,
> Our stitching and unstitching has been naught,

a 'beautiful mild woman' herself answers him,

> To be born woman is to know,
> Although they do not talk of it at school—
> That we must labour to be beautiful.

The answer is less about labour than about purpose, which fights softness and indolence. To Yeats, woman's beauty is a purpose, and it must take pains for it; and it is made by its pride in itself.

> She had been beautiful in that old way
> That's all but gone; for the proud heart is gone,
> And the fool heart of the counting-house fears all
> But soft beauty and indolent desire.

The beauty which poets and women make is one. It is the flower of their purpose.

And the flower does not grow without pains. Yeats writes again and again of the pains which his poems cost him. Now other poets have taken pains with their poems: Jonson was mocked for his great pains, Wordsworth made himself ill in writing some poems. But these poets did not make their pains the matter of their poems. Why does Yeats write poems about his pains?

The answer is that Yeats's pains do indeed sum his poems. Yeats's poems of this time are given their strength by his purpose. This forces the hard and exact word into its place. But this force is at odds with the writing. In the writing the senses always threaten to beat down the purpose. And this battle makes the pains of Yeats's writing. I have pointed to such a battle within Yeats's images. We can see it fought out at length in a later poem, *The Grey Rock*.

In *The Grey Rock* the goddess Aoife loves a young Irishman. He wants to fight in the Irish army; and to save him from hurt, the goddess gives him a pin which will not let him be seen. But the young man is ashamed of the charm before his comrades, throws it away and is killed. Now Aoife asks the gods to punish him because he has betrayed her. The matter of the story is the battle between purpose and the senses: between the young man's purposeful honour and Aoife's sensual love, between Aoife's purposeful hate and the drunken calm of the gods. And there is the same battle in the manner. The poem is broken by asides to say how hard it is to tell the story without being mastered by its winy images.

> We should be dazed and terror struck,
> If we but saw in dreams that room,
> Those wine-drenched eyes, and curse our luck
> That emptied all our days to come.
> I knew a woman none could please,
> Because she dreamed when but a child
> Of men and women made like these.

And the images themselves are godlike and sensual at once; and they end the story suddenly.

> Thereon every god stood up
> With a slow smile and without sound,
> And stretching forth his arm and cup
> To where she moaned upon the ground,
> Suddenly drenched her to the skin;
> And she with Goban's wine adrip,
> No more remembering what had been,
> Stared at the gods with laughing lip.

This is not an end. It is a running away from the end, in matter and in manner. Aoife is not answered when she forgets her purpose in drink. The story is not told when it is drowned in sensual delight. Yeats has taken the easy way out of the poem into the pleasure of the senses. In this moment Yeats has seen himself; and he has put down what he has seen more honestly than in some later poems in which he pities himself.

The purposes which play through *The Grey Rock* are honour and hate. Both are called out by love. At this time Yeats comes back to the theme of love in poem after poem, because he finds in it the most pressing purpose. He writes of the old love stories of Queen Maeve, of Cuchulain, and he says,

> O wandering birds and rushy beds,
> You put such folly in our heads
> With all this crying in the wind;
> No common love is to our mind,
> And our poor Kate or Nan is less
> Than any whose unhappiness
> Awoke the harp-strings long ago.
> Yet they that know all things but know
> That all life had to give us is
> A child's laughter, a woman's kiss.

This longing for the old loves is not new. Yeats took much of it from Swinburne; and it has some likeness to Housman's sadness. Housman also finds the old stories of love more moving than his loves. Housman also believes that he can hope for nothing from life but his loves. I quote a poem by Housman.

Tarry delight, so seldom met,
  So sure to perish, tarry still;
Forbear to cease or languish yet,
  Though soon you must and will.

By Sestos town, in Hero's tower,
  On Hero's heart Leander lies;
The signal torch has burned its hour
  And sputters as it dies.

Beneath him, in the nighted firth,
  Between two continents complain
The seas he swam from earth to earth
  And he must swim again.

Housman sees the steady loves of old fail as pointlessly as his loves. This is not what Yeats sees. Yeats ends the passage,

Who was it put so great a scorn
In the grey reeds that night and morn
Are trodden and broken by the herds,
And in the light bodies of birds
That north wind tumbles to and fro
And pinches among hail and snow?

His longing is for the purpose which has made great the little reeds and the light bodies of birds. In their scorn of the world he sees and seeks the greater end. This is what the old love stories tell him: that the steady purpose is greater than the world.

Yeats's search for purpose at this time is imaged in the form of the poems. These poems are abrupt and broken in their thought and in their verse. Each line and each sentence begins afresh, with a spurt which breaks again at the next line or the next sentence. I quote from *The Countess Cathleen*,

> What matter if your head's below your arms
> Or you 've a horse's tail to whip your flank,
> Feathers instead of hair, that 's but a straw,
> Come, share what bread and meat is in the house.

The verse strains to hold together beginnings and ends. But it cannot find the easy link in the meaning which should hold them. Yeats uses purpose to make this link. For purpose is the straining to link deeds or thoughts which the poet cannot make grow each out of the last. It makes by force a link between cause and effect where the link has broken. The poets just before Yeats were sure that they knew how effect follows cause. They took the link for granted. The poets after Yeats have been sure that they do not know; and some have done without the link. Yeats forcefully made his own link of purpose. In making it he made his poems. For his poems grow from the fruitful state when the poet sees beginning and end, and must make his own middle. They grow from Yeats's belief that the middle and the worth of poetry is an ideal purpose.

2

Unhappily, Yeats lost his belief in purpose. He lost it because he lost faith in his own purpose. When he lost it he lost the link which holds effect to cause in his poems. He found a new link at last in mysticism; and the growing of his mysticism is the change in Yeats's poems which we see most easily. I look behind it at his loss of faith in his purpose.

Yeats had found one ideal in poetry and in the greatest living: both are worthy because they are purposeful. He had not doubted that in writing poems he was also living well. He doubts it for the first time in the poems *Responsibilities*. The name warns us that Yeats is less happy in his work now. And the poems are bitter against those who have attacked his work. They begin with an apology for his work. Yeats asks pardon of his forefathers who fought at the Boyne, who

> Leaped overboard
> After a ragged hat in Biscay Bay:

who lived grandly. He asks their pardon,

> Pardon that for a barren passion's sake,
> Although I have come close on forty-nine
> I have no child, I have nothing but a book,
> Nothing but that to prove your blood and mine.

Yeats feels that he has fallen short of his forefathers. The barren passion which has made his poems is perhaps like their wilder acts. But it does not reach their best living: it does not make a child. To have written poems is to have failed the last test of great living. Yeats is about to set living against poetry, and to set it above poetry.

This opposition now becomes the theme of Yeats's poems. His early poems had indeed had a hint of it. They had set against one another the warrior and the saint, as symbols of living and poetry. In *Fergus and the Druid* each symbol had hankered after the other.

> *Druid:* No woman loves me, no man seeks my help,
>   Because I be not of the things I dream.
> *Fergus:* A wild and foolish labourer is a king,
>   To do and do and do, and never dream.

But this had been an equal and commonplace opposition: that every man would rather do another man's
work. Now Yeats makes the Druid's complaint in
earnest. He may give it the air of an equal choice:

> The intellect of man is forced to choose
> Perfection of the life, or of the work,
> And if it take the second must refuse
> A heavenly mansion, raging in the dark.
> When all that story's finished, what's the news?
> In luck or out the toil has left its mark:
> That old perplexity an empty purse,
> Or the day's vanity, the night's remorse.

But the air is false: the choice is weighted against the
poet. For Yeats finds the choice sad because he feels
that he has made the wrong choice. We see how the
verse which I have quoted lingers on the sadness of
the choice which he has made. Behind it Yeats is
looking wistfully to the choice which he might have
made. This wistfulness fills Yeats's later poems. Yeats
now longs for the life of the landed squires and of
Dublin gentlefolk: riding, loving, drinking; careless,
and winning all hearts. The longing is snobbish and
is jealous that stupid men are rich and handsome and
have many women.

> His great eyes without thought
> Under the shadow of stupid straw-pale locks,
> That insolent fiend Robert Artisson
> To whom the love-lorn Lady Kyteler brought
> Bronzed peacock feathers, red combs of her cocks.

And it leaves no doubt that Yeats is sorry that he has chosen to be a poet.

The opposition between poetry and living is not new. I have pressed it in this book. But it is new that a poet should use it to belittle poetry. It is new that he should set it out as a choice. For it is not a choice. To write poems is not to stop living. To live in the social world is not to give up the ideal of poetry. A choice can only be between two ways of living; and poetry is not a way of living. To make poetry against living a choice is to go behind the very opposition between them. For the opposition is between seeing poetry as its own standard, and judging it by the standard of living. To make poetry a way of living is to deny that it can be its own standard.

Yeats hides this contradiction by taking the choice a step farther off. 'The intellect of man is forced to choose' not between living and writing poems; but between the finished life and the written poem,

> Perfection of the life, or of the work.

This is the choice which Yeats has put in *Responsibilities*,

> I have no child, I have nothing but a book,
> Nothing but that to prove your blood and mine.

Good living is rounded by the child, which is its work and its symbol. And good living is the heirloom of the forefathers to whom Yeats writes this poem. Yeats is using symbols which give living a religious and ideal worth: for example, the breeding of children and the worship of forefathers make a religion in China. We may see the subtle confusion which Yeats is making by looking at his images. I have just quoted lines in which the child is the symbol of good living. I quote another poem which puts the same choice.

> Get all the gold and silver that you can,
> Satisfy ambition, or animate
> The trivial days and ram them with the sun,
> And yet upon these maxims meditate:
> All women dote upon an idle man
> Although their children need a rich estate;
> No man has ever lived that had enough
> Of children's gratitude or woman's love.

Here perfection of the life is to 'animate the trivial days', and its symbol is woman. Perfection of the work is to 'get all the gold and silver', and its symbol is the child. In two poems of the same time, then, Yeats uses the child as symbol in turn of each of the two opposed principles which each poem debates. The confusion is not chance. We can find it again in the other symbol which I have just quoted. This is the love of women; and is the symbol of great living. Yet Yeats writes of poetry,

You cannot give a body to something that moves beyond the senses, unless your words are as subtle, as complex, as full of mysterious life, as the body of a flower or of a woman.

He writes again of poetry,

The ancients and the Elizabethans abandoned themselves to imagination as a woman abandons herself to love.

Like the image of the child, the image of the woman has been doubled, so that it is the image at once of great living and of poetry. How does Yeats make peace between these again?

He makes it in a new way. When Peacock wrote *The Four Ages of Poetry* he claimed that poetry must be judged by its social usefulness. When Shelley answered in the *Defence of Poetry* he did not deny the claim. To Shelley also poetry and living were one, and poetry was to be judged as a kind of living. When Yeats writes of Shelley he steadily makes the least of this belief. He makes the most of the desperate rant at the end of the *Defence of Poetry* in which Shelley tries somehow, anyhow to make an ideal. Yeats writes of Shelley,

> He seems in his speculations to have lit on that memory of nature the visionaries claim for the foundation of their knowledge; but I do not know whether he thought, as they do, that all things good and evil remain for ever, 'thinking the thought and doing the deed', though not, it may be, self-conscious; or only thought that 'love and beauty and delight' remain for ever.

Yeats is turning Shelley's belief upside down. He is making Shelley say that poetry and living are one not because poetry is a kind of living, but because living is a kind of poetry. And this now becomes Yeats's own answer to the question, How are poetry and living linked?

Yeats's early poems saw in poetry an ideal worth of purpose. In some high moments, in love, in war, in beauty, this ideal could also give its worth to

living. Yeats lost the belief in purpose when social
and political bitterness mastered his poems. The bitterness made him belittle poetry and set it against great
living. When he came to link them again he put the
worth in living. This was now to be an ideal absolute
as poetry, and as lasting. Somehow, somewhere living
must leave a mark as beautiful and steady as a poem.
Yeats now finds his peace in this mysticism. He sums
it when he writes of an old woman whom he had
known young,

> All lives that has lived;
> So much is certain;
> Old sages were not deceived:
> Somewhere beyond the curtain
> Of distorting days
> Lives that lonely thing
> That shone before these eyes
> Targeted, trod like Spring.

The life in the world is only a moment in a lasting
life. And the lasting life, it seems, fixes that moment
when the living thing was most beautiful. Life of
itself has all that for which we hanker in the poem:
it is beautiful, absolute, planned, and lasting.

We have reached Yeats's mysticism by way of his
loss of purpose. Purpose had been the link from
beginning to end, from cause to effect in his poems.
When Yeats lost it he lost the link which the reason
makes. He found an unreasoning link in mysticism.
Above all in the mystic symbols he found the ravelling
of beginning and end which gives his poems their
knotty strength and speech. No images which the
poet has made can give this strength: for they can

give back no more than the poet has put into them. But the old symbols can suddenly give the poem its own meaning and its own end, beyond the thought of the poet. Yeats has stressed this power of the symbols.

It is only by ancient symbols, by symbols that have numberless meanings beside the one or two the writer lays an emphasis upon, or the half-score he knows of, that any highly subjective art can escape from the barrenness and shallowness of a too conscious arrangement, into the abundance and depth of nature.

And his poems are now made up of the symbols: the sword which is the soul; the blood which is the body; the gyre of change; the ideal round of the moon in which all change ends; the beggars who are the foolish living men and the fool who is the wise lifeless man; the tree

> That from its topmost bough
> Is half all glittering flame and half all green

in which the ideal and the living are set against one another and yet held together; the woman who is great living; Byzantium where the great life ends. We may take Yeats's two *Byzantium* poems as the models of these poems and of their mystic belief.

The first poem is *Sailing to Byzantium*. Here Yeats is old and he no longer has a place in the world of the senses. In the world of the senses

> Fish flesh or fowl, commend all summer long
> Whatever is begotten born and dies.
> Caught in that sensual music all neglect
> Monuments of unaging intellect.

But an old man must seek the other world where the monuments of unaging intellect stand. This other world is Byzantium. Yeats calls to the wise men of Byzantium,

> Consume my heart away; sick with desire
> And fastened to a dying animal
> It knows not what it is; and gather me
> Into the artifice of eternity.

Byzantium is an artifice. When he comes there Yeats will leave his old body and will become one with the works of art.

> Once out of nature I shall never take
> My bodily form from any natural thing,
> But such a form as Grecian goldsmiths make
> Of hammered gold and gold enamelling
> To keep a drowsy emperor awake;
> Or set upon a golden bough to sing.

In the second poem, *Byzantium*, Yeats speaks from Byzantium. Mere living is ended, and the work of art is set up.

> A starlit or a moonlit dome disdains
> All that man is,
> All mere complexities,
> The fury and the mire of human veins.

Aptly Yeats finds an image here,

> An image, man or shade,
> Shade more than man, more image than a shade,

which has within itself the work of art. It has the living force of a poem, which can call from the dead across the dead. For the work of art is a 'miracle, bird or golden handiwork': it can crow to the living, or it can scorn them in self-glory. But the work itself draws from the living before it leaves living to become the work of art: to Byzantium

> Blood-begotten spirits come
> And all complexities of fury leave,
> Dying into a dance,
> An agony of trance,
> An agony of flame that cannot singe a sleeve.

And Yeats suddenly sees the spirits come, riding the dolphins of human passion. They ride towards Byzantium where the goldsmiths hammer out the last beauty like a gong above the passions. Passion and ideal, all is at last bound in the images.

> Astraddle on the dolphin's mire and blood,
> Spirit after spirit! The smithies break the flood,
> The golden smithies of the Emperor!
> Marbles of the dancing floor
> Break bitter furies of complexity,
> Those images that yet
> Fresh images beget,
> That dolphin-torn, that gong-tormented sea.

3

Yeats has not stopped at this belief. The thought which drove him from the ideal of purpose step by step to the mystic ideal of living has driven him farther. When he first put aside the worldly life for the mystic life in *Sailing to Byzantium*, the mystic life was still a life of the mind. Byzantium was the town of monuments of unaging intellect. Yeats's heroes at this time were men of the mind, Swift, Berkeley, Burke. His soul asked him,

> Why should the imagination of a man
> Long past his prime remember things that are
> Emblematical of love and war?
> Think of ancestral night that can,
> If but imagination scorn the earth
> And intellect its wandering
> To this and that and t' other thing,
> Deliver from the crime of death and birth.

But the second *Byzantium* poem hints that there is a change in Yeats. Now he feels that Byzantium can only be reached astraddle on the dolphin's mire and blood. And soon the self comes to answer his soul,

> A living man is blind and drinks his drop.
> What matter if the ditches are impure?
> What matter if I live it all once more?
>
> I am content to live it all again
> And yet again, if it be life to pitch
> Into the frog-spawn of a blind man's ditch.

The image of the spawn speaks for itself. From now on Yeats sees the mystic life as a sexual life. He who had sailed to Byzantium because the sensual world belongs to the young in one another's arms now praises Byzantium because he finds there a spawning and sexual life more exciting than that which he has left.

> Crossed fingers there in pleasure can
> Exceed the nuptial bed of man;
>
> A nuptial bed exceed all that
> Boys at puberty have thought.

There 'Godhead on Godhead in sexual spasm begot Godhead'. The love of women has at last come into its own; for in Byzantium 'perfection of the work' does not seem to call the poet out of bed.

Yeats has taken his belief so far in his book *A Full Moon in March*. He will not go back from here. Everything he writes now is to say this: that the ideal lives because it is sexual.

> What can she lack whose emblem is the moon?
>
> But desecration and the lover's night.
>
> Why must those holy, haughty feet descend
> From emblematic niches, and what hand
> Ran that delicate raddle through their white?
> My heart is broken, yet must understand.
> What do they seek for? Why must they descend?
>
> For desecration and the lover's night.

Against any less sexual ideal Yeats says roughly,

> An abstract Greek absurdity has crazed the man—
> Recall that masculine Trinity. Man, woman, child (a
>   daughter or a son),
> That's how all natural or supernatural stories run.
>
> Natural and supernatural with the self-same ring are wed.
> As man, as beast, as an ephemeral fly begets, Godhead
>   begets Godhead,
> For things below are copies, the Great Smaragdine Tablet
>   said.

And Yeats was bound to reach this belief because it is the last belief on the path on which he has been driven. Yeats has been driven by the mystic images which have made his poetry and his belief.

The strongest of these images has been the image of the woman. His early poems saw love as an ideal purpose. His later poems saw love as the symbol of great living. And he also saw love as the symbol of poetry.

The ancients and the Elizabethans abandoned themselves to imagination as a woman abandons herself to love, and created beings who made the people of this world seem but shadows, and great passions which made our loves and hatreds appear but ephemeral and trivial phantasies.

This symbol could not be kept out of Byzantium. It was to be foreseen that Yeats's ideal there would at last be a sexual ideal.

I recall the 'passion' which Swinburne praised 'as of Gods chasing the daughters of men'. It was to be foreseen that Wordsworth's ideal of passion would become Swinburne's sexual passion. The thread runs on to Yeats. It was to be foreseen that Coleridge's ideal of life would become Swinburne's vague life. This thread also runs to Yeats. I quote the end of the sentence which I have just begun from Yeats.

But now it is not the great persons, or the great passions we imagine, which absorb us, for the persons and passions in our poems are mainly reflections our mirror has caught from older poems or from the life about us, but the wise comments we make upon them, the criticism of life we wring from their fortunes.

The beginning of the sentence recalled Swinburne's passions and sexual images. The end recalls his dislike of Matthew Arnold. Yeats has not held to the barren 'pure' poetry of Swinburne. But he has taken from Swinburne Coleridge's ideal of an abstract life which our life shadows. He has made the abstract life more real by making it sexual,

> Clip and lip and long for more,
> Mortal men our abstracts are,

because he has gone past Swinburne to Blake. He reads Blake thus,

The reason, and by the reason he meant deductions from the observations of the senses, binds us to mortality because it binds us to the senses, and divides us from each other by showing us our clashing interests; but imagination divides us from mortality by the immortality of beauty, and binds us to each other by opening the secret doors of all hearts. He cried again and again that every thing that lives is holy, and that nothing is unholy except things that do not live—lethargies, and cruelties, and timidities, and that denial of imagination which is the root they grew from in old times. Passions, because most living, are most holy—and this was a scandalous paradox in his time—and man shall enter eternity borne upon their wings.

The first sentence is just. The rest is Blake read by Coleridge's meaning of imagination, not Blake's; and it is not Blake but Yeats.

Swinburne, Housman, and Yeats are the poets who praised Blake most. Each saw Blake as the poet who held most strongly to poetry. This is what Swinburne means when he writes of Blake,

To serve art and to love liberty seemed to him the two things (if indeed they were not one thing) worth a man's life and work; and no servant was ever trustier, no lover more constant than he.

This is why Housman finds Blake 'the most poetical of all poets'. And this is why Yeats takes his passionate symbols from Blake. We may give the same praise to these three poets. More than any poets since Blake they held strongly to poetry as they understood it. Nevertheless Swinburne was a disorderly and a wasted poet, and Housman was so thin and silly that he can hardly be called a poet. Yeats is the best of the three, and is the best poet of a hundred years. He alone of the three has put the theory which branches through them into a form in which it can be granted or denied, but in which it stands alone.

Coleridge made a beginning for this theory when he saw poetry as the gift of that imagination by which man gives his life to nature. Swinburne made of this an abstract life and false passion which allowed him to hold to the social being of poetry and to 'pure' poetry at once. His theory is divided against itself, and it shirks both the world and poetry. Housman gives this theory again whimsically in *The Name and Nature of Poetry*. Housman also cries for 'pure' poetry, Housman also tests it in the feelings, and Housman also ends in contradiction.

Yeats takes the theory farther. He makes it bolder and richer. I have followed his path step by step. At the first step, Yeats finds the worth of poetry in purpose; and this worth also marks the best living. I see in this a likeness to the worth of Virtue in Sidney, of Nature in Dryden, which I have taken as model. But Yeats loses this worth. He loses his own purpose in bitterness at having missed the life of rich and handsome men. For a time Yeats sets poetry against living, and belittles poetry in the contrast. From now on Yeats finds worth in living; and when he grants poetry a worth again, the worth is that of a kind of living. In this belief, the place of purpose is taken by mysticism. For since living is to be an ideal, it must be as free from the mere happenings of a lifetime as is a poem. Yeats's ideal at this step is a mystic life of which one lifetime is only a sensual moment.

> Things out of perfection sail,
> And all their swelling canvas wear,
> Nor shall the self-begotten fail
> Though fantastic men suppose
> Building-yard and stormy shore,
> Winding-sheet and swaddling-clothes.

The work of art and the great life are one in this mystic life in Byzantium.

But Yeats's belief is driven one step farther. His Byzantium has an ideal life: but since this is a life, it must be like life. 'Things below are copies.' Therefore the mystic life must have loves and passions like ours; it must be sensual and sexual, it must shirk the mind. Yeats had given up the sensual life in *Sailing to Byzantium*. Now he clutches for it again, and his fear is to lose it.

> God guard me from those thoughts men think
> In the mind alone;
> He that sings a lasting song
> Thinks in a marrow-bone;
>
> From all that makes a wise old man
> That can be praised of all;
> O what am I that I should not seem
> For the song's sake a fool?

I pray—for fashion's word is out
And prayer comes round again—
That I may seem, though I die old,
A foolish, passionate man.

This does not merely give the senses their place in the poem: it puts the senses at the core of poetry. Yeats has now taken the social beliefs of the nineteenth century into mysticism. He has made the social life a life of the senses alone. He has made this life of the senses an ideal. And he has made poetry and living one within this mock ideal. He has made the life of the senses the ideal from which poetry takes its worth.

I see in this the last anti-poetic faith. It dwarfs the social beliefs of the nineteenth century as Yeats dwarfs the poets of the nineteenth century. Yeats claims that he has taken his faith from Blake. But Blake wrote of a less sensual poet than Yeats,

I see in Wordsworth the Natural Man rising up against the Spiritual Man Continually, & then he is No Poet but a Heathen Philosopher at Enmity against all true Poetry or Inspiration.

Blake would have read Anti-Christ in Yeats's faith. For Yeats stands against the line of poets whose ideal was poetry. And he stands away from the little poets of the nineteenth century who tried to fit poetry into a social use. He is a poet of great living and of the senses. Yeats is a poet great enough to stand against poetry.

LIST OF QUOTATIONS
AND INDEX

LIST OF PASSAGES QUOTED

The sources of some quotations are given in the text: the others are briefly listed here. The quotations are taken from the earliest texts which have authority, where these are available to readers.

The quotation on page 5 of the FOREWORD is taken from Dryden's *Essay of Dramatick Poesie*; the first quotation on pages 7 and 123 from his *The Hind and the Panther*; that on page 14 from Sidney's *Defence of Poesie*.

The quotations from Sidney in the essay on PHILIP SIDNEY are taken from the *Defence of Poesie* or from *Astrophel and Stella*; those from Gosson from *The Schoole of Abuse*. The quotations from Milton on page 23 are taken from *Eikonoklastes*. The couplets from Blake on pages 48 and 64 are taken from *Auguries of Innocence*.

The quotations from Shelley in the essay on PERCY BYSSHE SHELLEY are taken from the *Defence of Poetry* or from *Prometheus Unbound*; except the last quotation on page 86, which is taken from *Queen Mab*. The quotations from Peacock are taken from *The Four Ages of Poetry*.

The quotations from Jonson in the essay on JOHN DRYDEN are taken from *Discoveries*; except the first quotation on page 94, which is taken from the Dedication of *Volpone*. The first passages on page 96 are quoted from Dryden's *Parallel of Poetry and Painting*; the quotation from Dryden on page 98 is taken from the Preface to the *Fables*; the first quotation on page 101, and the last on page 110, from the Epistle Dedicatory of *The Rival Ladies*; the last quotation on page 104 from the *Apology for Heroique Poetry*; the quotation on page 105 from the Defence of the *Essay of Dramatick Poesie*; the quotation on pages 106 and 124 from the Dedication to *Examen Poeticum*; the quotation on page 108 from the Preface to *Annus Mirabilis*; the first quotation on page 110 from the Preface to *All for Love*; the quotation on page 112 from the Prologue to *Aureng-Zebe*;

the second quotation on page 122 from the *Song for St. Cecilia's Day*; and the first quotation on page 124 from the Elegy *To Mrs. Anne Killigrew*. The other quotations from Dryden are taken from the *Essay of Dramatick Poesie* or from *All for Love*; those from Shakespeare from *Antony and Cleopatra*. The quotation from Sidney on page 104 is taken from the *Defence of Poesie*; and that from Pope on page 107 from the *Essay on Criticism*.

The quotations from Wordsworth in the essay on WILLIAM WORDSWORTH for which other sources are not given are taken from the Preface to the second edition of the *Lyrical Ballads*, from *Tintern Abbey*, or from *Intimations of Immortality*; except the first quotation on page 141, which is taken from *The Prelude*, and the quotation on pages 151 and 154, which is taken from his Letter to John Wilson. The quotation from Dryden on page 132 is taken from the Preface to *Sylvae*, and the quotations from Coleridge on pages 136–7 from the *Biographia Literaria*.

The quotations from Coleridge in the essay on SAMUEL TAYLOR COLERIDGE for which other sources are not given are taken from *Dejection* or from the *Biographia Literaria*; except quotations on pages 163–7, 172–3, 177, and 181–2, which are taken from his *Shakespearean Criticism*. The quotation from Pope on page 178 is taken from a letter to H. Cromwell.

The quotation from Swinburne on page 189 of the essay on ALGERNON CHARLES SWINBURNE is taken from *Itylus*; the quotations on pages 190 and 201 from his essay on *Byron*; the third quotation on page 192 from his essay on *Coleridge*; the second quotation on page 206 from *St. Dorothy*, and the third from *Laus Veneris*; the quotation on page 207 from *The Garden of Proserpine*; and the quotation on page 208 from his essay on *Shelley*. The other quotations from Swinburne are taken from his essay on *Wordsworth and Byron* or from *Tiresias*. The quotation from Arnold on page 195 is taken from his essay on *Wordsworth*; and the first quotation on page 200 from Coleridge's *Biographia Literaria*.

The second quotation from Housman on page 220 of the essay on ALFRED EDWARD HOUSMAN, the first quotation on page 221, and the first quotation on page 222, are taken from *Last Poems*. The first quotation on page 223 is taken from *More Poems*. The other quotations are taken from *The Name and Nature of Poetry* or from *A Shropshire Lad*. These quotations are made by permission of the Trustees of the late A. E. Housman's estate, and of the publishers, namely The Richards Press, Messrs Jonathan Cape Ltd, and the Cambridge University Press.

The quotations from Yeats on pages 231–7 of the essay on WILLIAM BUTLER YEATS are taken from *Later Poems*; the third quotation on page 238, the third quotation on page 243, and the first and second quotations on page 244 from *The Tower*; the third quotation on page 246, the quotations on page 247, the first quotation on page 249, and the second quotation on page 251 from *A Full Moon in March*. The other quotations from Yeats for which no source is given are taken from *The Winding Stair and other Poems* or from his essays *Ideas of Good and Evil*. Permission to quote complete poems has been given by Mr Yeats and by his publishers Messrs Macmillan. The quotation from Housman on page 235 is taken from *More Poems*; that from Swinburne on page 249 from his essay on *William Blake*; that from Blake on page 252 from the margin of his copy of Wordsworth's *Poems*.

INDEX

CAMBRIDGE: PRINTED BY W. LEWIS, M.A., AT THE UNIVERSITY PRESS